BEE COUNTY COLLEGE
DATE DUE

NOV 3 1982		

19872

WILD BILL AND HIS ERA

[JAMES BUTLER HICKOK]

WILD BILL *and* HIS ERA

The LIFE & ADVENTURES
of
JAMES BUTLER HICKOK

By

WILLIAM ELSEY CONNELLEY
Late Secretary of the Kansas State Historical Society

With
INTRODUCTION by
CHARLES MOREAU HARGER

NEW YORK
COOPER SQUARE PUBLISHERS, INC.
1972

Originally Published 1933
Published 1972 by Cooper Square Publishers, Inc.
59 Fourth Avenue, New York, N. Y. 10003
International Standard Book No. 0-8154-0413-1
Library of Congress Catalog Card No. 76-187842

Printed in the United States of America

Contents

iii

Introduction

HISTORY ever has found difficulty in establishing the actual happenings surrounding notable personages. Their contemporaries, if not passed from the scene, however sincere their relation of events, frequently disagree, because each has lacked a complete picture of events. Legend and literary license have added incidents bristling with strange exploits but without real foundation. This is particularly true of so colorful a life as that led by James Butler Hickok, frontiersman, soldier of fortune, peace officer and hero of many a weird tale of imaginary adventure.

His very title, "Wild Bill," smacked of tempestuous undertakings, of daring deeds, of fearsome conflicts in the untamed reaches of the plains. His experiences are not far back in the years. Only seven decades have passed since his activities spread their audacious record over the Middle West. Yet live many who knew him, who daily watched his performance of duty, who had a part in his enterprises and should possess an accurate vision of his character and his accomplishments. Seemingly there should be a clear and definite understanding of the man and of his history. But even here, in my home town, where he walked the streets, preserved the peace, aroused the populace by killing in the pursuit of duty and was familiar to every citizen, some of whom still survive, are varied interpretations of his performances and his motives.

Because Hickok was a part of the development of the plains country through its period of transition from a limitless expanse of grass and stream and straggling settlement to the beginnings of economic and social advancement and because he stood out spectacularly in the happenings of those times, it is desirable that the story of his life and the part he played should be preserved while material therefor is obtainable.

No historian was so well qualified for this task as William Elsey Connelley. His was a type of mind fitted to delve into the most complicated labyrinth of tradition and find the truth. Painstaking, sure of his statements, gifted with a pleasing style, and trained by his position as Secretary of the Kansas State Historical Society to allow no assertion to go unchallenged, he entered upon the writing of this book with a sincere purpose—to give an authoritative history of "Wild Bill" Hickok. It was a task of years, during which he sought every possible item of value and interviewed men and women who had been acquaintances and associates with the frontier hero. He took nothing for granted and sought to create from original sources a delineation accurate in every detail.

Mr. Connelley searched the records to present a sane, convincing portraiture of "Wild Bill" as he was. When the work was nearly finished he was called from his earthly labors and it is fortunate that his notes were in the hands of his daughter, Mrs. Edith Connelley Clift, who had assisted him in the undertaking. She has rounded out the story with skill and appreciation, giving to it the same fidelity of treatment with which it was begun and so nearly completed by its author.

The literature of the Great Plains, already voluminous, can be written fully only by including the epoch-making deeds of those outstanding figures who participated in its notable events. Whether conquerors, builders, adventurers or keepers of the peace, they had their place in the establishment of a mighty empire. This is the life-story of one of these—an actor on that stage whose name will stand permanently in the roster of those having a thrilling part in the marvelous transformation of untenanted spreading prairies into a land of homes, of farms, of cities, and of fine American citizenship.

CHARLES MOREAU HARGER

Abilene, Kansas

List of Illustrations

Editor's Note

MY FATHER, William Elsey Connelley, died on July 14, 1930. He left behind him an unpublished biography of Wild Bill Hickok. The manuscript contained too great a mass of material to be crowded into any one book. With the instinct of the true historian to preserve all data, he had been unable to leave out many interesting details. Naturally, the result was a too cumbersome book, for no skill could arrange such a quantity of facts between the covers of the average volume.

It has been with trepidation that I have undertaken to edit the manuscript. Much that is valuable has been removed, and much that was left has been condensed. To know what to take out and what to keep was a problem. Minor happenings and incidents, told to illustrate diverse traits of Wild Bill, or simply related for their own interest, have been dealt with ruthlessly. Military campaigns and Indian affairs of great importance have received slightest mention.

Some scouting experiences, some few examples of Wild Bill's courage and skill as a marksman have been retained. But the list could be expanded thrice over, easily. The majority of these stories are so marvelous as to be almost incredible. But in every instance, they have been given by honest and highly respected men, some of whom were Wild Bill's close personal friends and fellow-scouts. Many of them are vouched for by several witnesses. There is some reliable authority for every fact here presented.

I have found among my father's correspondence, many hundreds of letters, asking when the book Wild Bill would be available to the public. So, for my father's sake, and for the sake of those who desire the real story of the Great

Plains scout and Marshal of Border bad towns, I have made this effort. If I have blundered at times, please forgive me.

I have, so far as possible, condensed the few notes kept. I do not feel that a mass of notes and references helps a book much. But I was compelled to place a few at the close of the book.

When the book was being written by my father, I worked on it, under his direction. Several of the chapters here given are my writing. No two people write alike—or see through the same eyes. So, naturally, these chapters differ from those written by my father. But, seen through his eyes or mine, Wild Bill remains the same fascinating personality. I hope, together, we have been able to re-create him, his environment, and his times, for you.

And I hope you will find both entertainment and instruction in this story of frontier days and ways.

EDITH CONNELLEY CLIFT

Lawton, Oklahoma
1933

Preface

IN THIS work will be found an account of historical events on the Western frontier. This portrayal is necessary to a comprehension of the services of Wild Bill. He cannot be properly shown in any other setting.

I lived in communities where first-hand information of Wild Bill could be obtained. In Wyandotte County, Kansas, I met some of the Red Legs who had served with him in many a scout. At Springfield, Missouri, I found his comrades-in-arms—old soldiers who had been with him, and were familiar with his services during the Civil War. There I met Mrs. Talahina Allen, widow of Wild Bill's most intimate associate in his war service—a "Pin" Indian—converted to anti-slavery views at the Mission of Rev. Jones, a few miles west of Cincinnati, Arkansas. For nearly thirty years I have lived at Topeka. Here I have met many men who knew Wild Bill after the Civil War, among them Colonel Edward C. Little, of Abilene; Colonel H. C. Lindsay, of Topeka; Robert M. Wright, one of the founders of Dodge City; J. B. Edwards, of Abilene; and many others. I knew Alexander Majors, Colonel W. F. Cody, and Dr. Albert Morrall. On the Southern side I had a personal acquaintance with Cole Younger, Frank James, Captain William H. Gregg, Ves Akers, "Babe" Hudspeth, Ben Morrow, Morgan T. Mattox, and many guerrillas who served under Quantrill.

In the capacity of Secretary of the Kansas State Historical Society I have had free access to its marvelous store of information on the West. I have spent forty-two years gathering material for this book. The first statement which I secured was from Theodore Bartles, long a chief of the Red Legs. Often in this service he was with Wild Bill in desperate and thrilling situations and later they were together on scouting expeditions on the Great Plains.

Bartles was one of the few men to whom Wild Bill opened his heart. It was to Bartles that Bill made his first complaint of the account of the Rock Creek affair as written by Nichols and published in *Harper's Magazine*, February, 1867. He repudiated some things in that account to both Bartles and Colonel H. C. Lindsay.

I discovered that there was really little in print which was authentic by which to check Wild Bill's life. There was some truth in Buel's book, but much that he recorded was pure invention. Buel pretended that he wrote from Wild Bill's diary. He did no such thing—for the very good reason that Bill never kept a diary.

Wild Bill never killed without cause and justification. Some men he only kicked out of the "bad" towns. They were insignificant scoundrels—minor criminals who lived by petty larceny. Away from Bill they could boast of what they had done to him—or what they had seen others do to him. But those who listened oftentimes believed they were hearing the truth and for that reason these stories tended to increase rather than diminish. For a generation past they have appeared in sensational newspaper articles.

William E. Connelley

Rooms, Kansas State Historical Society,
    January 7, 1928

WILD BILL AND HIS ERA

WILD BILL AND HIS ERA

CHAPTER I · *Wild Bill Himself*

THIS is the story of Wild Bill. Here he walks the earth again, a living, breathing man. On the wide-stretching stage of the Great Plains, he once more takes up his life of scout, of plainsman, of "bad-town" marshal, of gallant, debonair adventurer. He flashes across the colorful history of the West— a picturesque and brilliant figure.

Wild Bill is Youth incarnated—vital, bold, quick to judge, and swift to punish; imperfect and often at fault, but living a hard life and one of the deadliest peril—with the courage and fearlessness of a brave gentleman.

Wild Bill's achievements—his marksmanship, his services as a soldier and scout, his "cleaning up" of bad border towns, these in themselves hold great interest. But, apart from the man and from all those myriad traits that make up his extraordinary personality, they are, after all, merely more historical data. Vivified by the bravery and adventurousness of Wild Bill himself, these feats may approach the splendid simplicity and grandeur of an epic.

. . . .

Wild Bill was a trifle over six feet in height, and though not massively built, he was strong, with an effortless, smooth-flowing strength. He possessed the steel-sinewed, swift-

1

flashing grace of the trained fencer. From his broad shoulders to his slender ankles he tapered with a fine symmetry. He had a chest measure of forty-six inches, and the slender waist of a girl. He carried himself proudly erect. On horseback he was a figure so matchless that Mrs. Custer,[1] ignoring the General's other scouts, devoted pages to his description.

To one who has known of Wild Bill's deeds, but who has had no knowledge of his personality, his pictured face is always an astonishment. To expect the grim, square-jawed, battle-scarred countenance of the usual fighter, and then to gaze into a grave, steady-eyed, sensitive face—this is ever a surprise. But it is often true that a man's nature stands forth on his countenance: many of the seemingly contradictory traits of Wild Bill's character may be reconciled by one who holds his shadowed likeness and searches it closely. The honesty and iron will of the man is written large, to be read. His friendliness and grave courtesy are most apparent.

Wild Bill, in his day, was called the handsomest man west of the Mississippi. His eyes were blue—but could freeze to a cruel steel-gray at threat of evil or danger. The man who incurred his displeasure, glimpsing them briefly from under half-shut lids, saw them as cold, greenish, steel-gray. Much has been said of Wild Bill's hair. It was golden-brown, matching the color of his drooping mustache. This long hair gave him something of a girlish look. But this was most contradictory. In reality, long hair was a badge of manhood and courage, for it was worn as a challenge to any Indian who thought himself a brave—a challenge to come and take it. It was temptation and defiance flaunted carelessly and constantly in the face of vicious and treacherous enemies.

Wild Bill was not an ignorant man. He wrote and spoke good English. The writers who put in his mouth crude, foolish jargon, purporting to be a dialect, do him wrong.

The man was in many ways an anomaly. In a period when

dirt and slovenliness was a generally accepted state, he re-
belled against it absolutely. He kept himself immaculate and
well groomed. He bathed and shaved every day, when he
could in any way obtain the means for these luxuries. He
had an actor's passion for fine clothes. The garb he wore when
out on the plains was picturesque. But, in from scouting expedition, he shed his outdoor costume of fringed and beaded
buckskin and decked himself in truly gorgeous raiment. One
contemporary, who appreciated the vivid picture he created
in the streets of the rough little border towns, wrote:

I have seen him in a Prince-Albert coat, checkered trousers, a silk waist-
coat embroidered with colored flowers, and over his shoulders, a cape with
a flowered silk lining. He took as much pride in his boots as in his wealth
of blond hair. They were made to his order in Leavenworth, and I have
known him to pay as much as sixty dollars for a pair. The tops were of
black patent leather, embroidered in various devices of curves and spirals,
and the heels were two inches high.

Wild Bill allowed himself one more dashing note of color—
a broad sash of embroidered scarlet silk, in which he carried
his two ivory-handled, silver-mounted revolvers. His head
covering changed according to his occupation and the season.
But oftenest, he wore a soft, dark, broad-brimmed hat of
felt. And about his footgear he displayed a naïve vanity. His
feet were small and slender for his size, and he shod them by
turn in soft, exquisitely beaded moccasins, or the high, expensive boots just mentioned.

All this is for Wild Bill's appearance—his face and form
and dress. It must all be kept in mind to give a correct and
balanced understanding of the man and his most personal
characteristics.

First, and the foremost of all the qualities that distinguished him, was his bravery. He would not have lived long
had he been a heavy-footed, reckless fool rushing unthink-
ingly into needless danger. He was always careful, with the
caution of a clever man who knew himself to be in constant

peril, and was accordingly on guard. He knew with absolute certainty, that he walked the earth surrounded by the most deadly danger. He knew that one false move, one split second's hesitation, one instant's relaxation of his vigilance—and his life was forfeit. So he went watchfully, courageously, prepared, armed for instant action. But he walked the streets of Abilene, where death lurked in waiting every minute, as confidently as a king traversing his capital. For him "fear" was a word without meaning. It was simply a quality he lacked.

He feared no living man. And he feared no dead one. Asked once how he felt over the bad men whom he had shot, he answered:

As to killing men, I never think much about it. I don't believe in ghosts, and I don't keep the lights burning all night to keep them away. That's because I'm not a murderer. It is the other man or me in a fight, and I don't stop to think—is it a sin to do this thing? And after it's over, what's the use of disturbing the mind? The killing of a bad man shouldn't trouble one any more than killing a rat or an ugly cat or a vicious dog.

Wherein Wild Bill stated his creed. He felt that his conscience was clear—that crime deserved and should have instant punishment. And indeed, such punishment was a positive necessity if lawlessness was not to check civilization at the Western frontier.

Wild Bill never boasted of his attainments. Low voiced, and courteous, he was willing to join freely in general conversation. But he became at once shy and inarticulate on the subject of his own bravery and skill. Faced with admirers, he blushed and stammered and fled.

Wild Bill lived in an atmosphere of recklessness and violence and bloodshed. And it would be foolish to deny that he derived great pleasure from his ability to control with relentless, iron-handed justice the wild, violent, law-breaking element whom he ruled so absolutely.

But, on the other hand, he had a longing for quiet and

peace. He liked to fish, lounging on the green bank beside some sleepy stream. Alone, or with some friend, he passed dreamy, silent hours, watching the ripple of the little waves. The blaze of crimson sumac against the misty blue of Indian summer, the great star-studded chalice of the midnight heavens, the bending flow of wind-stirred prairie grass—he spoke of the delight these things gave to him.

Wild Bill knew the Great Plains as Daniel Boone knew the great woods. He knew the Plains as a scout must know them —knew them with a painstaking familiarity that took into account every little sign that told its tale of passing Indian or animal, or friend or foe who went that way. The prairies were a great book whose pages, illegible to most, were plainly printed for him. Which is why Custer called him the greatest scout.

One of Wild Bill's most persistent traits was his liking for children. A family of four children living in Topeka and attending school there were astonished and flattered at the interest he gave them. He sought them out, and bestowed upon them much attention. He showed them how to ride and patiently demonstrated his marksmanship for their amusement. He encouraged the boys of the family to visit him at his hotel. This they did, constantly, to the great disgust of the room-clerk. In his apartment he fed them on stories and an indiscreet amount of candy. He would stop his progress to discuss gravely the fine points of some mongrel puppy with its young proud owner. He would desert the company of men to play in a ball-game with a gang of half-grown youngsters. A woman whose husband was station-agent at Chapman, a little town near Abilene, tells of Wild Bill's devotion to her baby boy. The train stopped at that point for water, and he never failed to take advantage of the stop to come to the station for a romp with the baby.

In the men whose daily concern is with the gravest matters

of human life and safety there are often left absurdly young and boyist traits. Wild Bill retained a fund of impish mischief and humor that won him the approbation of all youngsters. In from some dangerous scouting trip across the Plains, he often hunted up some woman with a reputation for good cookery, and bribed her to make for him a couple of large and juicy pies. These he carried carefully away, and he was sometimes seen sitting, unabashed, on a curbstone, devouring a half of one of his trophies with the greatest relish. Often some urchin, straying along, was invited to join the feast, and the two consumed the pie in solemn enjoyment.

As to Wild Bill's morals, one writer says of him: "Hickok's morals were much the same as those of Achilles, King David, Lancelot, and Chevalier Bayard, though his amours were hardly as frequent as David's or as inexcusable as Lancelot's."

Wild Bill found relaxation and enjoyment in cards but he seldom drank. He knew too much depended on perfect control of mind and body to risk upsetting his nerves by drink. He did not have any prejudice against drinking. He never tried to dissuade any of his friends from it, and he "treated" those who cared to drink whenever courtesy demanded it. No one has ever said, with any truth, that Wild Bill hunted for trouble. But, as he himself phrased it: "I won't be put upon!" Knowing this, bad men out searching for excitment drew the line at hunting him up.

Wild Bill said of the frontier: "No Sunday west of Junction City, no law west of Hays City, and no God west of Carson City." Which was true. It was a short and vivid summary of the situation he was called on to confront. And it produced a situation so incredible as to be without parallel in history—one man holding in subjection, by the sheer strength of his iron will, a town full of desperate criminals all eager for his blood.

Any man who by his own force and fearlessness beats the dark forces of savagery and crime, so that civilization may be free to take another step forward on her march of progress —is he not the greatest and truest type of the frontiersman? Such a man was Wild Bill.

He was not only a pioneer, but he carried within himself that onward-thrusting, high-flaming spirit of the Pioneer of all time. He typified that pioneer, enduring danger and hardship that in his wake might follow peaceful farmers and merchants; that where he had passed might spring up villages and towns.

Wild Bill is a figure unapproached in American history for daring, for picturesqueness, and for romance. Had he lived in France, a few centuries earlier, he would have been a swordsman, a blithe soldier of fortune, light-hearted, swift, and dangerous as a lightning flash, worthy to have been adopted kindred adventurer by the Three Musketeers, to have made their trio a quartette.

But a man must live out his life in the century in which Fate drops him. So Wild Bill, in his setting of pioneer life of the Great Plains and the rough border towns of the frontier, is still kin to that joyous and doughty brotherhood of man, who, down through the ages, sought heroic adventure and valiant achievement. He is in very truth, a gay and gallant gentleman.

CHAPTER II · *Wild Bill's Marksmanship*

Ever since the invention of firearms the ability to shoot quickly and accurately has been deemed a preëminent accomplishment.

Wild Bill loved the six-shooter. With one of these in hand he was master of any situation. In rapidity and dexterity of its use he stands above all others.

It must be stated here that Wild Bill never shot from the hip, various writers to the contrary notwithstanding. And Wild Bill never filed down the catches which held the pistol cocked until he had to hold and release the hammer with his thumb. He honed these catches down with great care until his pistols were easy on the trigger. Wild Bill could twirl his pistol on his trigger-finger, firing every time the handle came up into his grasp.

In Topeka Wild Bill did some fine shooting. Mr. Marshal saw him throw up a coin and shoot it to pieces before it hit the ground. George M. Stone saw him shoot a row of holes close to the edge of the brim of Buffalo Bill's hat when it was spun up into the air.

While he was marshal of Abilene two men committed a murder. They fled, and Wild Bill came up with them at Solomon. As Bill burst into one door of the saloon they ran out at the opposite door. When Bill came out following after them one was running up the street and the other down the street in the opposite direction. Bill fired at both men simultaneously and killed them both. This was witnessed by Andrew Platner, a good citizen still living. He was a boy on

8

his way to school. He told the coroner that Bill killed both
men with one shot. When the coroner laughed, the boy said
he had heard but one shot. The pistols had been fired in opposite directions so nearly at the same time that the boy
had heard but one report. This was in 1871. Letter of Andrew
Platner to author.

It is a satisfaction to find a reliable record of the ability
of Wild Bill to do accurate and rapid shooting. Such a record
was made by the late Robert A. Kane, a man as well known
in sporting circles as any in America. Mr. Kane was an
authority on firearms and their use. In *Outdoor Life* for June
1906, he gives the following account of Wild Bill's shooting:

Along in the '70s Wm. F. Cody (Buffalo Bill), Wm. A. Hickok (Wild
Bill) and Texas Jack, as members of Buffalo Bill's "Prairie Waif" Company, played a three-nights' engagement in Milwaukee, Wisconsin.
Several of the local marksmen, including myself, called on the celebrities
at their hotel, where in a little social session shooting and shooting methods
were discussed. Mr. Hickok treated us with great courtesy, showed us his
weapons, and offered to do a little shooting for us if it could be arranged
for outside the city limits. Accordingly the early hours of the afternoon
found us on our way to the outskirts of the city. Mr. Hickok's weapons
were a pair of beautifully silver plated S.A. .44 Colt revolvers. Both had
pearl handles and were tastefully engraved. He also had a pair of Reming-
ton revolvers of the same caliber. The more showy pair of Colts were used
in his stage performance. On reaching a place suitable for our purpose,
Mr. Hickok proceeded to entertain us with some of the best pistol work
which it has ever been my good fortune to witness.

Standing on a railroad track, in a deep cut, his pistols cracking with the
regularity and cadence of the ticking of an old house clock, he struck and
dislodged the bleaching pebbles sticking in the face of the bank, at a distance of about 15 yards.

Standing about 30 feet from the shooter, one of our party tossed a quart
can in the air to a height of about 30 feet. This was perforated three times
before it reached the ground, twice with the right and once with the left
hand.

Standing midway between the fences of a country road, which is four
rods wide, Mr. Hickok's instinct of location was so accurate that he placed
a bullet in each of the fence posts on opposite sides. Both shots were fired
simultaneously.

Located midway between two telegraph poles he placed a bullet in one of them then wheeled and with the same weapon planted another in the second. Telegraph poles in this country run about thirty to the mile, or 176 feet distant from each other.

Two common bricks were placed on the top board of a fence, about two feet apart and about 15 yards from the shooter. These were broken with two shots fired from the pistol in either hand, the reports so nearly together that they seemed but one.

His last feat was to me the most remarkable of all: A quart can was thrown by Mr. Hickok himself, which dropped about 10 or 12 yards distant. Quickly whipping out his weapons, he fired alternately with right and left. Advancing a step with each shot, his bullets striking the earth just under the can kept it in continuous motion until his pistols were empty.

In *Outdoor Recreation* for November 1912, Mr. Kane writes:

On the single occasion which the writer was priviledged to witness the methods of Mr. Hickok in handling his six-shooters, I was deeply impressed with his almost exasperating deliberation. No matter how elusive the target, even when shooting at objects tossed in the air, he never seemed hurried. This trait was, of course, natural, and in part due to his superb physique and superior mentality, which, combined with and supplemented by his methods of practise and free, wild life in the open, developed in him that perfect coördination of hand and eye which was essential to perfect mastery of the one-hand gun. . . .

The writer has himself seen Mr. Hickok shoot, using a Colt single action revolver in either hand, firing simultaneously or alternately, and I am prepared to believe any story of his skill or prowess that does not conflict with the laws of gravitation and physics.

I have seen Wild Bill fire two shots simultaneously, using both hands, at stationary targets, and alternate shots with either hand at moving objects, for a limited number of shots, and score with each shot. It was while giving an exhibition of his skill with a six-shooter that I saw him hit a quart tomato can while in the air, with two single action Colt six-shooters. He did not seem to be hurried and I feel sure he could have fired another shot with his left hand.—By courtesy and permission of *Outdoor Life*.

CHAPTER III · *The Hickok Family—*
Wild Bill Leaves Home

THE Hickok family was founded in America by William Hickcox. When he came from England to the Colony of Connecticut is not known, but he was in New Haven in 1643. No trace of him is found after 1648. He had two sons, Joseph and Samuel. Joseph was born about 1650, and died at Woodbury in 1687. The date of the birth of Samuel has not been ascertained, but an inventory of his estate was made February 28, 1694, and he must have died a short time before that date. The descendants of Joseph and Samuel Hickcox lived principally in Connecticut, but they spread all over New England, many of them moving to Vermont.

In Vermont the Hickoks prospered. They lived principally in the northwestern part of the state. In the history of that commonwealth much is set down of their services in the War of the Revolution—on occasion, under General Ethan Allen.

No effort has been made to trace the descent of James Butler Hickok from any of these Revolutionary soldiers. But it is established that the Hickok family is one of the oldest and most honorable in America. It was of pure Saxon blood, and Wild Bill bore the traits and characteristics of the Ancient Saxons.

The parents of James Butler Hickok were natives of Grand Isle County, Vermont. The Butler family moved from North Hero to Potsdam, in New York State, about 1827. Polly Butler was then almost eighteen. She and William

11

Alonzo Hickok were lovers, and he soon followed the Butler family to New York State. There he married Polly Butler. Two children were born to them while living there. In 1833 the Hickoks loaded their possessions into a covered wagon and set out for Illinois. In the same year they settled at Union Grove, Putnam County. Jume 16, 1834, they moved to Bailey's Point, and in November 1836, in company with the Reverend N. Gould and Isaac Fredenburgh, they moved to Granville. Here they remained only a few days, going on to Troy Grove, where they arrived before the first of December.

Troy Grove is in La Salle County, and here, in 1836–37, they erected a frame dwelling. This house stood upon a prairie and fronted east. It was half a mile from the timber growing along Little Vermillion Creek. Later, this place became the site of a village named Homer, and the dwelling house was in the southeast corner of block thirteen of that town, by the official survey and recorded plat.

Six children were born to William Alonzo and Polly Hickok, as follows: Oliver C., born in New York State in 1830; Lorenzo B., born in New York State in 1832; Horace D., born in Putnam County, Illinois, in 1834; James Butler, born in La Salle County, Illinois, May 27, 1837. His mother named him for her father, James Butler; Celinda D., born in La Salle County, Illinois, in 1839; Lydia M., born in La Salle County, Illinois, in 1842. She married a man named Barnes and lived in Northwest Kansas. She died there.

The father, William Alonzo Hickok, died at the home in La Salle County, May 5, 1852, and the mother, Polly Hickok, died there in 1878.

The life of James Butler Hickok at home was that of all boys living in frontier settlements in the Great West. Illinois was at that time largely a frontier community. In the vicinity of Troy Grove there were such schools as could be found in pioneer settlements all along the American frontier. The boy attended these schools, and obtained in them a good elementary education.

But the supreme delight of James Hickok was hunting. He wandered through the bodies of timber skirting the prairie streams of Illinois in search of the small game which remained to his day. His weapons were of the poorest quality, but he was soon the best hunter in his community, although his hunting was in opposition to the wishes of the family. When he was about twelve years old he secured in some way, perhaps by the sale of furs, a good rifle and a Colt's revolving pistol. With these weapons he was a much more efficient hunter. He became the best shot in his part of Illinois.

William Alonzo Hickok established the first store in Troy Grove. This store was in a room of an old tavern called the Green Mountain House. It was in the block in which Hickok had built his residence. He operated this tavern as well as the store. The Green Mountain House was a station on the Underground Railroad, and Hickok was a strong Abolitionist. The next station on the Underground was Wedron, sometimes called Panton's Mills. Hickok had a team of Kentucky horses for use on the Underground, for it was necessary to go swiftly from one station to another, as the slave-carriers were often pursued by officers. When there was room in the wagon Hickok took some of his sons with him on these trips. James, later to become famous as Wild Bill, was often huddled into the wagon-box with the fleeing negroes. The pursuing officers always opened fire on wagons containing fugitive slaves, and young Hickok learned early in life what it was to be shot at.

After the death of his father it was necessary for James to apply himself more steadily to work. He drove freighting teams for village merchants, did chores and odd jobs about town, and finally secured a position as mule-driver on the

Illinois and Michigan canal. Many of those in the service of
the canal company were of the rougher sort. James soon
learned that, however pacific his personal feelings, he must
battle, to hold his own.

A driver, Charles Hudson, with whom James was associated, had often humiliated him. One day, he said something
which angered the boy. James, having reached the limit of
forbearance, attacked Hudson so suddenly and so vigorously
that he had him badly beaten before the bully realized that
there was to be a fight. In their struggle they fell into the
canal. When James was pulled out of the water, Hudson had
not yet been fished up. The boy, believing that his antagonist
was dead, and fearful of the results in case that should be
true, immediately ran away. He went to the City of St.
Louis where he remained a week or two along the levee.

This was in the summer of 1855, and the troubles in
Kansas occupied the public mind. People from all parts of
the West were on the road to Kansas. Hickok became one of
this ardent, restless throng, and he took passage for Leavenworth, on a boat now said to have been the *Imperial*. His
landing there was a very commonplace event, not the spectacular advent into Kansas Territory which it has been
pictured.[1] James Hickok, looking for a job, was given work
by Richard Budd, who lived just west of the town of Leavenworth. While working there, James avoided both town and
fort.

We next hear of Hickok in Johnson County, Kansas. There
are yet living Kansas people who saw him there in 1855 in
what is now Monticello Township. This county was a part
of the country set aside for the Shawnee Indians, who had
been removed from their eastern homes to a reservation on
the south side of the Kansas River.

Living near Mill Creek, in that township, was a white
man named John M. Owen (often found written Owens) who

was born in Tennessee in 1813. He came to Missouri in 1833, and in 1836 he came to Kansas, living with the Kansas Indians at Mission Creek in the western portion of the present Shawnee County. In 1839 he left the Kansas Indians and went to live with the Shawnees on that wonderfully beautiful Kansas River bottom opposite Bonner Springs. In 1840 he married Patinuxa, a Shawnee woman. The Shawnees did not adopt him, as was the usual custom, and in 1849 he moved out of the Indian country to go to California. He returned later and bought an improved tract of Shawnee land from one Tooley, a Shawnee Indian. After this purchase the Shawnees adopted Owen into the tribe. Owen and his Shawnee wife had only one child, a daughter, Mary Jane Owen. She is said to have been a very intelligent girl and of fine appearance. She was a good cook and an excellent house-keeper. Hickok was in love with this Indian girl and it has been said married her, but this he did not do. She later married one S. Harris, sometimes spoken of as Dr. Harris. On the map of Monticello Township, published in 1874, the land allotted to Mary Jane Owens stands in the name of S. Harris.

Hickok was at that time a tall slender young fellow, noted for his activity and his good nature. He was employed by a man named Williams to break prairie in the summer of 1856. Fred McIntyre, now living at Olathe, was a small boy at that time. He remembers seeing Hickok breaking prairie. Hickok was always very fond of children, and he permitted McIntyre to ride on the beam of his breaking plow.

At this time, Kansas engrossed the attention of the Nation. In November 1854, there had been held an election for a delegate to Congress. There were three candidates to be voted for, one of whom was John W. Whitfield, chosen by the Pro-slavery party and the Missourians. Mr. Whitfield was elected. A total vote of 2871 votes had been polled, of which 1729 were cast by Missourians who invaded Kansas for the

purpose of carrying the election. The citizens of Kansas were
outraged, but still greater humiliation awaited them. Governor Reeder called the election for the Legislative Assembly
for the twentieth of March 1855, and the Missourians along
the border, who became known as Border Ruffians, again
invaded Kansas in force, voting at all the precincts, and
electing the legislative body for the Territory of Kansas.

This body may have been in session when young Hickok
arrived in Kansas. It met first at Pawnee, a town which had
been surveyed by Governor Reeder and his associates, on a
portion of what is now the Fort Riley Military Reservation.
An old stone building, erected to be the Capital, still stands
as the ruined and solitary monument to the efforts of Governor Reeder to found a capital city for the Kansas Territory. The people of Kansas revolted against the actions
of this legislature. They designated it the "Bogus Legislature." It met at Pawnee, and adjourned to the Shawnee Mission, three miles southwest of Westport, now Kansas City,
Missouri. Among the resolutions adopted near the close of
this legislature was the following:

That it is the duty of the Pro-slavery party, the Union men of Kansas
Territory, to know but one issue, slavery; and that any party making or
attempting to make any other is, and should be held, as an ally of aboli-
tionism and disunion.

The slave code enacted by this legislature was atrocious.
Together with the resolution defining the issue, it was a
challenge to the Free-soil people of Kansas, and to free institutions. The result was civil war in Kansas. When James
Hickok arrived, the battle lines were forming.

CHAPTER IV · *Early Life in the West*

WILD BILL and John Owen were in the Free-State army organized by General Lane in 1856. They were with Lane on the thirtieth of August when he dispersed Atchison's forces at the crossing of Bull Creek in Johnson County. For this service in the Free-State party Owen lost his citizenship in the Shawnee Nation. On the fourth of September, Hickok was one of the guard standing about Lane in Lecompton when the pro-slavery forces were thrown into confusion and fled, leaving the town in possession of the Free-State men.

Hickok accompanied Colonel Lindsay when he took a drove of horses and mules to Kansas City early in 1870. As they passed through the ruined town of Old Franklin a few miles east of Lawrence, he said to Lindsay that he had seen a thousand Border Ruffians camped in that vicinity in the summer of 1856 and had assisted in driving them back to Missouri.

We get brief and imperfect views of the services of Wild Bill in the Free-State cause. We see enough, however, to know that he was active on the Free-State side. He was in all the major operations of General Lane in the summer of 1856, and perhaps in other operations of Free-State forces. Kansas was the battle-ground for the destruction of slavery and little regard was had for law in that turbulent period.

By September 1856, it was unsafe to travel in the Territory. The Missourians returned to wreak vengence on Lawrence and other Free-State towns. They were prevented

17

from accomplishing this by Governor John W. Geary. These
bands of Missourians crowded all trails and roads. Burning
houses lighted up the nights, and, quite literally, dead men
lay along the highways. To avoid extermination the Free-
State people rallied under General James H. Lane who had
won renown in the War with Mexico. Under his leadership,
the Missourians were repelled. By the summer of 1858 the
land was practically redeemed to the Free-State men, though
disorders continued until the close of the Civil War.

Mr. Bayless S. Campbell, now of Gillead, Nebraska, was
a resident of Kansas at that time, and he states that he first
saw Hickok at Highland, Kansas, in 1857. General Lane
made a Free-State speech there in the fall of that year.
Campbell lived there at that time, and he saw two men dis-
mount from their horses and lie down on the grass near some
stone-masons who were building the foundation of a hotel.
These two men were General Lane's bodyguard, and one of
them was Hickok.

Campbell saw Hickok with Lane at Grasshopper Falls,
now Valley Falls, in Jefferson County. Lane there made a
very bitter speech, flaying the Border Ruffians as no other
man could. He made his speech from a wagon-box, the wagon
having been drawn up there for the speaker's stand. A Border
Ruffian standing near-by, pulled a pistol. Hickok drew a
pistol and covered the Ruffian, who put up his weapon and
slunk away.

On March 22, 1858, occurred the election for township
officers in Kansas Territory. Those elected for Monticello
Township, Johnson County, were: R. W. Williams, Chair-
man of the Board of Supervisors; W. Mason, Supervisor;
John Owen, Supervisor; J. B. Hickok, Constable. All these
officials were commissioned by Acting Territorial Governor
James W. Denver, the commissions being dated April 21,
1858. Politics entered into this election, and this was the

Free-State township ticket. Hickok took the duties of his office seriously and was painstaking in their discharge. It was a matter of pride with him, and his election seems to have marked the beginning of the second period of his residence in Johnson County.

Given here are extracts from letters written home by Hickok from Monticello in 1858. These letters are full of the spirit of the boy he was. They show that he was beginning to assume all the responsibilities of the man he was to become. He was living at the Tavern in Monticello (see following chapter) at this time but was also living part of the time in a cabin on his claim. He was mowing and putting up prairie hay for the horses at the Tavern in Monticello. The letters are boyish and carelessly written:

MONTICELLO, August 14th, 1858.

DEAR BROTHER:

I have neglected answering your letter. But I beg to be excused this time and I will give my excuse. I went to Lecompton as a witness, and also on business of my own. I have the best lawyer engaged to tend to my claims that there is in the Territory. There will be no danger but what I will get my claim.

Mother mentioned something about drinking and gambling in her letter. Well now, I will tell you what is a fact. I have not drank a pint of liquor in a year, and I have not played for a cent in twice that time.

I have been making hay for four or five days. I have got it all stacked ready for rain. Just got through about half an hour ago. I think that Guy Butler [his cousin] will write to you that I am mighty poor company. He thinks I talk less than any man he ever saw. I wanted to talk to him, but I would get to studying, some times two hours, if he did not say anything. I sit some times two hours and think about one thing and another without speaking even when the house is full of people.

I want to tell you that the Delaware lands are coming into market. I live right close to these lands and when they do come in I am going to have a wipe at them sure.

There is one section over there that I would like to have for us four brothers. There are about one hundred acres of timber on the section and the rest beautiful prairie that can't be beat in the country.

JAMES B. HICKOK

Monday, August 16th, 1858.

I will write a few minutes while dinner is cooking. I have been and served three summonses this morning. There has been 25 horses stolen here within the last ten days by two men by the name of Scroggins and Black Bob. They have nary one been taken yet but I think they will be run up soon to the top of some hill, I guess where they won't steal any more horses.

I am going out to see Guy next Sunday. He is turning out an awful mustache and goatee. But I think my mustache and goatee lays over his'n considerable. The fact of it is, his'n ain't nowhere.

I went to see my girl [Mary Owen] yesterday and ate black berries that she picked Saturday. You ought to be here to eat some of her biscuits. She is the only one that I ever saw that could beat Mother making biscuits, and I ought to know, for I can eat a few you know. I have got to go this afternoon and subpoena a dozen witnesses, so I will quit, eat my dinner, and go.

JAMES BUTLER HICKOK

MONTICELLO, Friday Evening, August 20th 1858.

I have raked and put up two ton of hay in about an hour and a half and now I will write a little more if I can think of anything more to write. I have got to mow one hundred tons of hay yet, and maybe two hundred. I don't know yet really how much I have got to mow.

HICKOK

Monday 23rd.

Celinda said that she would send a letter that she got from Oliver, but I did not get it when I got here. I shall look for it yet. If I don't get it you must write what news there was in it. I should like to know when she is coming home for if she should come home soon you could look for me shortly after.

Monday Night, 10 o'clock.

I quit writing to go hunting. I have just returned and got my supper and thought I would write and tell you what luck I had. One young buck and two turkeys, which I carried home on my back. And now you may think I am tired, which I surely am, but however, being tired and wet while sitting by the fire, I might as well write as not. There is plenty of game here, more than there was on the other side of the river. Geese are plenty here in the fall.

JAMES

On the back of the letter is written as follows:

If you want to know how I spent my Fourth I can tell you. I split 225 stakes and "packed them out of the *Bresh*" as a Missourian would say, and it was an awful hot day here sure. if I am a judge of small matters.

Monday Morning, 23

I would have finished this letter yesterday but I was not at home. I was over at John Owens. I go there when I get hungry just as I used to come home to mother's to get something to eat.

Mary cut off a lock of my hair yesterday and said for me to send it to my mother or sisters. If she had not thought a good deal of you all she would not have cut it off, for she thinks a great deal of it. At least she is always combing and curling it, that is, when I am there. [This shows that Wild Bill got the idea of letting his hair grow long from the Shawnee Indians when living with them as a boy.—W.E.C.]

JAMES B. HICKOK

I received a letter from Celinda Friday. Mary got it and read it for she reads every letter that I get and said she would answer it for me and tell Celinda all about that girl she spoke of and tell her her name. It is noon now and I am waiting for my dinner. I promised Guy that I would come out to Olathe and see him last Sunday but it rained all day and I did not go.

JAMES B. HICKOK

CHAPTER V · *Adventures on the Santa Fé Trail*

THE town of Monticello was laid out in 1857. A new road was marked out from Leavenworth to the Valley of the Kansas River. Its first station was at the Delaware Baptist Mission, now the village of Maywood, in Wyandotte County. From that point the road followed easy grades to the site of Edwardsville. A little below Edwardsville was a ferry on the Kansas River, set up by the Chouteaus and known as "Chouteau's Ferry."

The site for Monticello had been selected for the reason that at that point the road from Wyandotte intersected the road from Leavenworth. From Monticello the road ran west up the Kansas River, and at Topeka turned southwest, reaching the Old Santa Fé Trail. John M. Reed was one of the Town Company, and in 1857 he erected a hotel at Monticello. This hotel became one of the famous hostelries of territorial Kansas. One of Reed's daughters was still living in 1925, and she described to the author, life at Monticello.

One day she and her brother, who were sitting on the front porch shelling peas to be cooked for dinner, saw a young man coming slowly down the road from the east. He bore a bundle, swung from a gun over his shoulder, and he was limping badly. He stopped at the porch, sat down on the steps, and began to talk to the children. He said he was hungry, and that he had just come up from Westport Landing, which point he had reached the day before on a steamboat. He had slept at night by the roadside, and his breakfast had been a rabbit which he shot and cooked in a small frying-pan. This frying-pan, a knife or two, and some salt were wrapped in two blankets, which, strapped together, made the pack which he carried. His lameness was caused by a badly bruised heel which had been rubbed by his boot. Mr. Reed came along while these young people were shelling the peas. Hickok inquired if he might remain at the hotel until he could travel, and do whatever work he was able to perform to pay his bill. He said that he had decided to go on to the Rocky Mountains. Mr. Reed said it would be all right for him to remain at the hotel.

Where was Hickok coming from when he first appeared at the Tavern? He had evidently been some distance away from Johnson County and had returned on a steamboat. There are statements, one in the letter of a Mr. Campbell, that Hickok assisted in getting a shipment of Sharps rifles up the Missouri River. It may have been that he had just accomplished this when he limped into Monticello with a bruised heel.

Or it may have been at this time that Hickok had been set upon by some ruffians at Leavenworth. The account of the affair was preserved by Herbert M. Stanley in his *My Early Travels and Adventures*, though he made Hickok say he was twenty-eight years old.[1] It was early in 1858, and Hickok was but twenty-one, perhaps only twenty, when the killing occurred.

Miss Reed (Mrs. Smith) said that the young man gave his name as Will Hickok, and that he was never known by any other name while he remained at Monticello. He was always most agreeable and helpful and would do cheerfully anything he found to do. In a month or two he began to have charge of the stage horses, and the oversight of the barn. Soon he was given complete charge of the stables and of the stage horses when they came in and went out. It was his business to have a fresh team ready to be hitched to the stage when it arrived. He frequently rode about the country between hours for stage arrivals, attending to his duties as constable. At this time he was holding a claim near-by, and he visited the Owen home often.

After Hickok had been in the service of Mr. Reed at the tavern three or four months, he was called upon to drive the stages if any driver should be sick or incapacitated in any way. He drove the stages to Lawrence, Tecumseh, Topeka, Council Grove, Leavenworth, Wyandotte, and other points on the line.

Independence, Missouri, was long the "jumping-off place" of the West. There the caravans were formed for the over-land trade with Mexico after 1830, and for almost half a century long trains drawn by oxen or mules left that old border town to traverse the Great American Desert. Their first objective was Santa Fé, and the ancient way over which they took their course was known as the Old Santa Fé Trail. It was over this Great Trail across the Plains that Hickok first drove a freight wagon, and later, the stage-coach carrying mails and passengers. It required bravery and skill to be a good driver. And the transportation companies refused to consider any applicant of whose absolute trustworthiness there was the slightest doubt.

The Old Trail, always ascending as it wound to the West, reached the eternal hills in the upper courses of the Arkansas. There, turning up the River of Lost Souls (Purgatoire— now corrupted to Picketwire), it climbed the heights known as the Ratons. The way was often hundreds of feet above the streams, winding about the dizzy ledges and shoulders of rocky promontories. In some places the road might be so narrow that the passenger in a stage-coach drew away from the window in breathless terror, appalled to see that he was seemingly suspended in mid-air over a yawning abyss.

[PILGRIMS OF THE PLAINS, FROM AN OLD PRINT]

The first stages over this line left Independence in May
1849. The team for each coach consisted of six mules, and
every stage was guarded by eight men. The cargoes of the
caravans of wagons carrying freight consisted of goods in demand in New Mexico. A freight-train consisted of from
twenty-five to forty wagons.[2] To each of these wagons were
hitched five yoke of oxen, and toward the end of the freighting era there were six yoke of oxen to each wagon. To manage a train of forty wagons, fifty men were usually required.
When oxen were used, the driver walked beside them, when
mule-teams were used the driver rode on the wagon.

One day a west-bound freight caravan of thirty or forty
wagons stopped at the Tavern. A driver of one of the teams
had fallen out of the service, and there was a vacancy which
the captain of the train urged Hickok to take, and which he
finally decided to accept. All the children in the neighbor-
hood cried when it was known he was leaving.

It must have been late in the summer or in the fall of 1859
that he left Monticello. Soon he became one of the trusted
drivers for the stage company; and was in charge of stations
and driving stages as far west as Santa Fé, New Mexico. In
fact, he drove the stage over Raton Mountains and into
Santa Fé in 1859 and in 1860. It was not a matter of great
difficulty to drive a stage over a prairie road, but in crossing
mountains with stages, danger was always present. These
stages were very high, and their construction permitted the
body to sway back and forth as they rolled along. When the
road ran above a cliff or gorge, it required great care in making turns and going around curves to prevent their toppling
over. But the passengers were never afraid to ride with
Hickok. When he drove into Santa Fé, he entered with a flour-
ish, and raised as much dust as he could. He took a mischievous delight in sending the lazy inhabitants scurrying out of
his way.

An important event of Hickok's employment on Old Santa
Fé Trail was his meeting with Kit Carson, the hero of his
childish imagination. He often met Carson in Santa Fé, and
sometimes found him on the trail. They became good friends.
Carson introduced Hickok to the underworld of Santa Fé.
The United States Hotel was the first point of interest to
which Carson carried him. In the bar-room there was a cos-
mopolitan crowd: Santa Fé traders and their customers, engaged in animated bargaining; trappers and hunters from the
south ranges of the Rockies beyond Taos, armed with Bowies
and Hawkins rifles, and wearing fringed buckskin; teamsters,
freighters, travelers, and native greasers. There was a din of
conversation, a jargon of tongues, and snatches of songs.
There was constant serving of liquor and the clink of glasses.

From this point they traversed the narrow streets of the
squalid quarters, coming finally to the principal gambling
house of Santa Fé. The room was long and narrow and the
ceiling low. There were slits for windows on one side, and it
was without a floor save the earth. On each side of the room
stood three tables. These were the "banks" and were piled
high with American, Spanish, and Mexican gold and silver
coins. At each "bank" lay a number of bowie knives, der-
ringers, and revolvers ready for instant use in case any cus-
tomer made a disturbance when he lost his money. At the
end of the room opposite the door was a roulette table.

Before reaching the roulette table, Carson and Hickok
stopped a moment at the monte section. In charge of this was
one Señora Doña Barcelo, who was a notorious New Mexican
character of the time. She was impressed by Hickok's fine
appearance, and called out "Carramba! Let the handsome
young American win!" This was spoken in Spanish to one of
her dealers. Hickok made a small bet and won. He made
another bet and won. He continued to win until his gains
amounted to several hundred dollars.

From this point Carson and Hickok went to a dance hall near the plaza. A fandango was just beginning as Carson and Hickok entered. Soon a violent altercation rose between two young Mexicans for the honor of the first dance with a girl. As the dance was already in progress she became impatient and ended the dispute by selecting the one she preferred. The rival left the room without a word, his face as black as midnight.

"Well, that little argument is settled," Hickok said.

"Just wait and see," replied Carson. When the music ceased, another Mexican approached the successful dancer and said that someone outside wished to speak to him. He should have known better, but he stepped outside; and a long narrow knife, wielded by his rival, was instantly thrust into his heart. This murder was regarded as a matter of course, and caused little excitement among the dancers. But Carson touched Hickok on the shoulder and said they had better leave before the usual riot broke out. Hickok remembered and sometimes mentioned his first night in the underworld at Old Santa Fé. (See *The Trail*, Denver, Jan., 1926, xviii, pp. 9–11.)

One cold winter day, Hickok was driving a stage east, drawn by three spans of mules, over the Raton Mountains. He had come through the Raton Pass and was descending the mountain. At the head of a narrow defile, he met a freight wagon loaded with barrels of whisky going up. The road at that point was a glare of ice and the oxen kept their feet with great difficulty. The driver of the freight wagon feared trouble, and Hickok advised him to use great caution, saying that chains should be wound around the hind wheels of the wagon. The stage was loaded with passengers, and it was requiring all of Hickok's ingenuity to take it safely down the mountain, although he had the wheels wrapped with twist-link chains.

Hickok had gone about two hundred yards after passing
this wagon when he heard a commotion. Looking back, he
saw that some of the oxen had fallen and that the heavy
wagon was rolling rapidly down the trail, dragging the oxen,
some of which were being thrown high in the air. The wagon
was rolling down the trail at a fearful rate, and Hickok saw
that it would soon overtake and wreck the stage. The passengers, in a panic started to climb out of the coach. Hickok
shouted at them to stay in—their only chance for safety. He
put the mules to a rapid trot—an extremely dangerous thing
to do, in the condition of the road. It took almost super-
human skill to hold the swaying bouncing stage on the icy
trail, manage the slipping frightened mules, and gauge the
awful progress of the oncoming heavy freight-wagon. This
last gathered constantly increasing speed. He flogged the
mules to greater speed.

There was a sort of broad turn in the road just ahead.
Hickok, realizing that there the wagon might either strike
the cliff and stop, or be thrown over into the chasm, dared to
hope that if he reached it the stage would be saved. And he
had just swayed, slipping dangerously, around the curve
when the wagon crashed into the protruding rock, wrecking
it completely. The impact threw the front part of the wagon
up into the air. One of the barrels was projected forward by
this upheaval and struck the rock just above the coach,
splintering the barrel and throwing the contents over the
stage.

Another barrel was coming down the trail, gaining im-
petus every second. Hickok realized that if it struck the
coach it would demolish it, and he flogged the mules to still
more insane speed. Leaping over a rock, the barrel seemed
bound to hit the coach. At that instant it struck the rocky
road between the hind wheels of the stage, burst open, and
the danger was over. The oxen were all killed, most of them

having their necks broken by being jerked and dragged down the steep and icy trail. When the wagon struck the cliff, it went over the precipice, taking the oxen with it. Hickok always said that that was the most frightful experience he ever had as stage driver.

In the fall of 1860, Hickok was delegated to take a freight caravan across the Raton Mountains. He had not been handling freight-trains for a year or more, but for some reason it became necessary for a man above the ordinary in ability and experience to have charge of this particular freight-train. Whether its cargo was of more than usual value, or whether there was danger of robbery, or whether the captain of the train first elected was incapacitated, is not known. Hickok met the train below Bent's Fort and took it safely over the Raton Pass. He spaced the wagons widely apart, escorting each one separately over the most dangerous parts of the road.

Once, in riding back to meet another wagon he came opposite a bunch of small bushy pines. A huge grizzly bear sprang out of the bushes into the road in front of him. Hickok's horse became insane from fright and was wholly unmanageable. The bear was determined on an attack. Hickok was thrown from his horse and in the fall one of his pistols dropped from the holster. Before he could rescue it the bear was upon him. As he emptied his remaining gun into her, he glimpsed her two cubs in the road and understood her rage. The shots did not check her furious assult and he drew his bowie knife, at the instant the bear struck him. He grappled with the infuriated beast, and the battle which followed is beyond description. He found it was safer to be up near or against the bear's body as she could not then do so much damage with her terrible claws, although she frequently struck him, inflicting dreadful wounds. He plunged the knife into her body frequently, but he made no apparent impression on the brute until, by a lucky stroke, he sank the knife deep in her belly and partly disemboweled her.

When the next wagon came up the driver found the bear lying on Hickok. He supposed both were dead, but Hickok was alive. His scalp was dreadfully torn, his left arm was crushed and still in the bear's mouth, and his breast and thighs were frightfully lacerated, but no vital spot had been touched. He was hurried over the mountain in a light wagon which was attached to the train, but no medical aid was secured until he arrived at Santa Fé. There he had what attention could be given him, but it was believed that he could not survive. His wonderful vitality saved him. The stage company had him brought out over the Old Trail in February. At Kansas City he had better medical attention, improved rapidly, and finally recovered.

[INDIANS ATTACKING A WAGON TRAIN, FROM AN OLD PRINT]

CHAPTER VI · *Wild Bill Kills McCanles*

THE first great tragedy enacted by Wild Bill was the
killing of McCanles at Rock Creek Station on the Old Oregon
Trail. McCanles had absconded while sheriff of Watauga
County, North Carolina.[1] When he left that country he took
with him a girl named Sarah Shull. The intention was to go
to the Pike's Peak gold fields, but a stop was made on the
way, and McCanles bought the Rock Creek Station. He
brought on his wife and family from North Carolina to Rock
Creek. When Wild Bill was sent there to recover from the
effects of his battle with the bear, many complications arose.
F. J. Wilstach, in seeking material for his work on Wild Bill,
discovered Sarah Shull and secured a statement from her. His
evidence is now available, and it convicts McCanles of those
things charged against him. It shows that he was the aggressor in the fatal encounter, and that he intended to "clean up"
on Wild Bill and others at Rock Creek Station.

David Colbert McCanles was born in Iredell County,
North Carolina, November 30, 1828. It is claimed that his
great-grandfather, David McCanles, came from Scotland and
settled in North Carolina in 1770. It is said that his grandfather, David McCanles, was a soldier in the Revolution,
but no record of that fact has been found. His father was
James McCanles, who moved to Watauga County, North Carolina, where he was fiddler, school-teacher, and cabinet maker.

McCanles was sent to private schools, and finally to a
military academy. In 1849, McCanles married Miss Mary
Green, of a Revolutionary family, resident also in Watauga

County. He was deputy sheriff from 1852 to 1856 under
Jack Horton, the sheriff. In 1856 he announced himself a
candidate for sheriff against Horton and was elected. This
step was in violation of his word to Horton, and resulted in
fierce personal physical encounters between the two men. He
held the office of sheriff until January 6, 1859, when he absconded.[1]

When McCanles and Sarah Shull (Kate Shell) left Shull's
Mills, the destination was Johnson City, Tennessee, on the
railroad. There horses, saddles, and bridles were sold to one
Joel Dyer and a train boarded for the West. At St. Louis
embarkation was made on a steamboat for Leavenworth,
Kansas. At Leavenworth McCanles secured equipment for
a trip across the Plains. As McCanles journeyed over the
Oregon Trail, he met many people returning from the Pike's
Peak country. They all told a story of discouragement. Gold
was indeed to be found in those regions, but in small quanti-
ties, and after much labor.

By the time McCanles had reached the Valley of the Blue
River, he had made up his mind to seek some different enter-
prise than that of gold digging. When he arrived at Rock
Creek Station on the Oregon Trail, he halted. Rock Creek
is in Jefferson County (then called Jones County), Nebraska.
It flows into the Little Blue River from the north, and is
about six miles east of Fairbury, the county seat. The Oregon
Trail crossed Rock Creek in Section Twenty-six, Township
Two, North, Range Three East. McCanles purchased a ranch
on the west side of Rock Creek, from one Newton Glenn.
This ranch was later known as West Rock Creek Ranch, and
was the only one at that time on Rock Creek.

During the summer McCanles built a ranch house on the
east side of the creek, where he dug a well which furnished
an abundance of water. He also built a toll bridge over
Rock Creek, which paid him handsomely. The east-side

ranch-house was called Elkhorn Station, and a pair of huge elk-antlers was nailed above the main entrance. McCanles used this station for the Overland mail, Stage, and Pony Express business, sending the freight wagons and the emigrant trains across the creek to the Rock Creek Station. The entire establishment was known by the general name of Rock Creek Station.

At this time, Sarah Shull learned that McCanles' wife and family would soon arrive from North Carolina.

Sarah Shull was then about twenty-six years of age, blue-eyed and dark haired. She was extremely attractive.

Dawson, in his *Pioneer Tales*, says: "They [the family of McCanles] took up residence in the east ranch-house, while Kate Shell [Sarah Shull] continued to be the mistress of the west side ranch-house."

In the meantime, the business enterprise of McCanles prospered. It is said that his total income was one thousand dollars a month. It was even whispered that he had so much money that he purchased a sufficient amount of gold to fill a large kettle which he buried at some point near Rock Creek Station, and the legend of the "Pot of Gold" may be heard there to this day.

McCanles was a strong virile character, a man of energy and initiative. He became a domineering spirit at Rock Creek and in its vicinity.

McCanles had developed a band of devoted followers— wild and reckless men, many of them voluntary outlaws. All of them did not remain at Rock Creek but held themselves within call. Some of them were in his service on the ranch, or herding cattle or horses on the prairies. At this time, McCanles stated that he had decided to return to the South and join the Confederate Army. This object in view, he disposed of his property at Rock Creek, and went to live on a ranch where that stream entered the Little Blue. It was off the line of travel and he thought his family would be safe there until his return.

In 1856, the town of Palmetto had been founded by men from the south. Palmetto was at the "Upper Crossing" of the Blue, where the Oregon Trail crossed the Big Blue River. It is now a part of the town of Marysville.

Dr. Albert Morral owned the townsite of Palmetto. He stated that he and all the other Southern men left Palmetto, immediately after Lincoln was elected president, to return to the south and fight. David McCanles, though apparently desiring to accompany them, remained behind, saying his affairs were not yet settled, and that he planned to follow within a short time. The men at Palmetto considered McCanles one of their number. The fight at Rock Creek in which he was killed prevented McCanles from becoming a Confederate soldier, in Dr. Morral's opinion.

McCanles was well known all along the Oregon Trail from Atchison and Leavenworth to Rock Creek. He often visited both Leavenworth and Atchison, and his associates were of the Southern element in those places.

In the spring of 1861, sometime in March, Wild Bill was sent to Rock Creek Station. He was recovering from the effects of his battle with the bear in Raton Pass, and many of his wounds were not healed. His left arm was still disabled, and it was with much difficulty that he could move it. McCanles was then in charge and assigned him to work as a helper at the stables. For some cause McCanles disliked Bill from the first and took every occasion to humiliate him. He gave him various nicknames, one of which was "Dutch Bill." He would seize Bill when there were crowds of men present and throw him down. Bill could not help himself then, for it was only with pain that he moved about at all. McCanles pretended that he was in fun, but it is possible that there was malice back of every movement.

After the removal of J. L. McCanles from the East Rock Creek Ranch, to the ranch on the Little Blue at the mouth of Rock Creek in the spring of 1860, David McCanles improved his property on the east side of the creek. He already had dug the excellent well there, and now he erected a commodious barn and a bunk-house—sleeping quarters. When these additions to the property were completed McCanles rented it to Russell, Majors and Waddell, who were then doing an immense freighting business and operating the Overland Stage line and Pony Express. When the firm took charge of the station it installed its own help. Horace Wellman, who had previously been in charge of the Big Sandy Station, was made the superintendent at East Rock Creek, and he, together with his common-law wife arrived early in May 1861, about two months after the coming of Hickok. When Hickok first came to Rock Creek, McCanles was making his improvements and was still in charge as agent and superintendent for Russell, Majors, and Waddell. He assigned the newcomer to a dugout cabin on the south bank of what is yet known as Wild Bill's Creek, and 150 feet southwest of the center of Section Twenty-six.

Soon after this McCanles sold out all his interests at Rock Creek, the Overland Stage Company taking over the East Station, but he still furnished hay for both stations. The consideration for the East Rock Creek Ranch had been arranged for payment in installments, seemingly monthly installments. Through the inattention of Ben Ficklin, superintendent, the payment for June was not made, and on the first day of July there was a default in the payment for that month. McCanles was impatient and much perturbed over the failure of the payment. He interviewed Wellman daily to see if the payments had arrived. Toward the last of June he had an extended and excited conversation with Wellman, who was only the agent and not responsible for the defaults. Wellman resented the insistence of McCanles and bad feeling was engendered.

McCanles believed that many persons would welcome his downfall. This was another reason why he was most anxious to close up affairs and get away. It was finally arranged that Wellman should go to Brownsville, on the Missouri River, and from the company's division office there get the money for the remaining payments to McCanles. In case the sum could not be secured in cash, McCanles agreed to accept "supplies" for the amount, should Wellman be able to make that arrangement. Wellman set out for Brownsville about the first of July, and Monroe, the son of McCanles, then twelve years old, went with him. With Wellman's departure, the situation changed at Rock Creek.

Sarah Shull was very much dissatisfied with the situation.

It is said that Hickock was swept off his feet by passion for Sarah Shull. However that may be it is certain that McCanles grew to regard Hickok with hatred.

When McCanles moved to the ranch on the Little Blue, Sarah Shull lived for a month or two at the West Rock Creek Ranch, McCanles warned Hickok to not cross the creek to the West Ranch unless he wanted to be killed.

When Wellman started to Brownsville, Hickok, at his request, left his dugout and went to live in the East Ranch-house to discharge the duties of the station-master. One day soon after the departure of Wellman, McCanles went to the East Ranch-house. He tried to terrorize Mrs. Wellman into giving up the Station if she could not make the defaulted payments. He roughly handled Hickok, who did not then resist, nor show his seething resentment.

Wellman did not return until the afternoon of the eleventh of July. He sent the boy Monroe home to tell his father the results of the journey. This intelligence greatly angered McCanles.

It was on the afternoon of July 12, 1861, that McCanles rode north from his ranch on the Little Blue to Rock Creek Station. He had been there in the forenoon and made a demand on Wellman for the Station and all the property connected with it. When this was refused, he told Sarah Shull he was going to "clean up" on the people at the Station that day. He must have known that this purpose involved violence. He was accompanied by his cousin, James Woods, his son Monroe, and James Gordon, a man in his service. He directed those with him to stop at the barn, and tie their horses there. He said he would confront Wellman and the bunch at the house alone. If his companions, left at the barn, should see or hear a serious disturbance, they were to come immediately to his assistance. McCanles was well armed, though it has been denied that either he or his men were armed. It would be a strange proceeding for a man who always went armed to discard his weapons when going expressly to confront "Wellman and his bunch" and "clean up" on the people at the Station. He directed his friends to come to his assistance when the trouble should start.

The Wilstach interview, before referred to, is here given:

Below are the answers to the questions asked Sarah Shull by Mr. Wilstach:

"Was money owed by Wellman the cause of the tragedy?"
"No."
"Were you in the cabin when McCanles was shot?"
"No. I was at my home two miles away."
"In your opinion, and from what you were told at the time, did Wild Bill kill McCanles in self-defense?"
"Certainly—yes."
"What makes you think this is true?"
"Because on the morning of the tragedy I heard McCanles say that he was going to clean up on the people at the Station."
"You say McCanles stole horses?"
"Yes, he stole horses."
"Were those horses for the use of the Confederate cavalry?"
"Yes."

No one blames Sarah Shull for denying that she was in the Station during the killing of McCanles and some of his gang. And it could not have been expected that she would admit that McCanles was going on West to operate along the Oregon Trail.

Why should he want trouble with Wellman? He was only
an agent. He did not owe anything on the Station. The
debt was not his affair. But, for McCanles' accommodation,
he had made a trip to try to get the payment. In his absence,
McCanles had terrorized his wife. And now McCanles was
threatening him.

The East Ranch-house was a structure about 36 feet long,
east and west, and about 18 feet wide, north and south. A
partition, midway of the house, divided it into two rooms.
This partition lacked some six feet of meeting, and so furnished entrance between the two rooms. The front door was
on the south and entered the west room near the partition.
The chimney and fire-place were at the west end. North of
the chimney there was another door, in the west end of the
house. There were two windows in the west room, one on the
north and one on the south. There were two windows in the
east room, one on the south and one in the east end. A calico
curtain, in two sections, strung on a lariat, shut off the view
of two beds standing against the wall of the east end.

McCanles stopped at the well, where he dismounted and
gave his horse water. He then went toward the west end of
the house. He was accompanied by his son Monroe, and he
met Wellman on the steps of the west door.

McCanles charged Wellman with duplicity, claiming that
payment could have been made, had Wellman wished. He
ended his tirade by insisting on prompt payment of all defaulted installments, or immediate possession of the premises.
He added that if possession was refused, he would take it by
force.

Wellman again reiterated what he had so often told Mc-
Canles, that he had been unable to secure the promised sum
from the company. But he could not give up the premises.
McCanles became threatening. In fear of his life, Wellman
left him and went into the house. He had no more than dis-

appeared inside than Mrs. Wellman, exasperated beyond en-
durance with McCanles, came to the door and defied him to
try to take the Station. McCanles refused to reply, stating
that he had come to settle with Wellman; his business was
with men and not with women.

At this juncture Hickok appeared at the door. He pushed
Mrs. Wellman aside and confronted McCanles. His appearance there surprised the enraged man, and must have had a
sort of sobering effect on him for he stopped to parley, something he would not ordinarily have done. He was not ready
to deal with Hickok at that moment. His turn would come
later. But he spoke to Hickok—

"What the hell have *you* got to do with this? But, if you
want to take a hand in it, come out and we'll settle it like
men."

Hickok did not answer McCanles at once. He was not
afraid, he was ready for action, now that the thin veneer of an
amicable relationship was cracked. He stood quietly regarding the angry and aggressive man on the steps. Mc-
Canles grew uneasy under that passionless quiet gaze, which
by its very blankness alarmed him. So he spoke, placatingly,

"We *are* friends, ain't we? I want to know. We have been,
ain't we, Hickok?"

"I guess so," Hickok answered slowly.

"Then," said McCanles, "send Wellman out here, so I can
settle with him, or I will come in and drag him out."

Apparently, Hickok complied with the request of Mc-
Canles, and stepped back into the room as though to get
Wellman.

McCanles left the west door and went around to the south
or front door, from which he had a view of the interior of the
whole house, except of that portion shut off by the calico
curtain. In the west room, the kitchen, was Sarah Kelsey,
who was a step-daughter of Joe Baker, and who had been at

one time in the service of McCanles. It is asserted by his friends that McCanles left the west door and went to the south door for the reason that these women would have been in the direct line of fire in case of shooting while he was at the west door—proof that he expected shooting and was prepared to shoot. McCanles stepped into the south doorway, from which position Wellman and Hickok were in his sight.

At any previous time up to his arrival on that day at the west door, McCanles could have gone in and confidently attacked both Wellman and Hickok. Now he could think of nothing better to justify his presence at the south door than to ask for a drink of water, clearly an excuse, for there was a bucket of water with a gourd-dipper in it on a table within two feet of him. Hickok left Wellman, went to this bucket, and dipping up a gourd-full of water, handed it to McCanles. After he had done this, he turned and walked rapidly back toward the curtain. McCanles had not wanted the water. He dropped the dipper and called upon Hickok to halt. Hickok disregarded this command. He stepped behind the calico curtain, which gave him the advantage.

At this instant, realization seems to have struck McCanles of the awful danger into which he had so thrust himself. But he was a brave man and almost instantly he called to Hickok to come from behind the curtain and fight fair. He added that if he did not do this, he would come and drag him out.

Hickok knew that to step from behind the curtain was to confront certain death, and he answered:

"There will be one léss ⸺ ⸺ ⸺ when you try that."

McCanles started forward.

Immediately a shot was fired from behind the curtains. The bullet went through the heart of McCanles, who staggered and fell backward in the yard. Notwithstanding his

[DAVE McCANLES, FROM A PHOTOGRAPH]

mortal wound, McCanles attempted to raise himself up and was aided by his son Monroe, who had run to his assistance. The stupor of death was passing over McCanles. Words formed on his lips, but were never spoken. His eyes glazed and he slipped through his son's arms and lay limp on the broad step at the door.

When Woods and Gordon heart the shot and saw Mc-Canles fall, they left the barn and ran at full speed to the house. Woods attempted to enter the kitchen door, which was the west door. Gordon ran to the south door. Woods was just entering the house, stepping over the threshold, when Hickok, who was standing partly behind the door, shot him twice with a revolver. Woods, mortally wounded, ran around the north side of the house, falling at the east end in a clump of weeds.

Gordon had reached the front door a moment after Woods had appeared at the west door. He came up just in time to see Hickok shoot Woods. This sight seemed to throw him into a panic and he turned to run, and, as he turned, Hickok fired at him, mortally wounding him. Gordon ran toward the barn, intending to secure his horse and get away, but as he went down the path Hickok shot him again.

Gordon turned about and fled down the creek for his life through the underbrush. Hickok, far in the rear, pursued him for some distance, firing until his revolvers were empty, but in the brush and leaves he could not see him distinctly and had to fire at random.

As Hickok returned to the ranch-house, Woods was found in the weeds just away from the east window, where he was killed with a grubbing-hoe, in the hands of a woman. (Very recently, Wellman has been charged with using the hoe.) In a moment the frenzied woman ran around the house to the front door brandishing the hoe. She cried out to Hickok, who was running to the Station to reload his weapons, "Come,

let's kill all of the —— —— ——." Horror-stricken, Hickok
tore the bloody weapon from her hands.

She had meant that the boy, Monroe McCanles, who was
still bending over the dead body of his father and did not
realize his danger, should be killed. The boy had been dazed
by the suddenness and horror of it all. But he glimpsed the
woman approaching him with the uplifted hoe. He leaped to
his feet and dashed away.

By that time there was a commotion about the two stations. A Pony Express rider named Doc Brink and George
Hulbert, a stage driver, were at the West Ranch-house, and
they hurried across the creek. John Hughes, who had pretended to be the friend of both McCanles and Hickok,
thereby causing neither to trust him fully, had been hunting
along the creek bottoms, and he arrived just after Gordon
had started to run down the creek. Hickok now called in
Joe Baker, who was one of the stock tenders at the barn, and
accused him of being a friend to McCanles and one of the
McCanles gang. Baker denied that he was a friend of Mc-
Canles or that he had intended to go away with him. Hickok
cocked his pistol with the intention of killing him, but his
step-daughter threw her arms about his neck and pleaded
for the life of the man. This caused Hickok to relent.

A bloodhound which had followed the McCanles gang up
to the station was set to trail Gordon through the underbrush along Rock Creek. The dog soon came up with him,
and Hickok and others arriving shortly after, found him
under a tree. One of the men in the gang shot Gordon, who
fell at the base of the tree.

Gordon was buried where he fell. Blankets were wrapped
around his body, and he was cast into the grave with his
boots on. Some local carpenter, or maybe two or three rough
workmen, including Joel Helvey, made a rude box in which
McCanles and Woods were placed. They were buried in this

box on top of what is known as Soldier Hill, where they remained for twenty years. The Burlington Railroad then came, and as the graves were on the right-of-way, the family caused the reinterment of the bodies at Fairbury Cemetery.

Sarah Shull left Rock Creek Station on the west-bound stage early on the morning following the tragedy. She was swallowed up by the vast and indefinite frontier to emerge only recently with no story of consequence to tell. She cannot be blamed for silence.

Hickok, Wellman, and Brink were arrested on the fifteenth day of July and arraigned on a charge of murder. Jefferson County, then Jones County, was unorganized, but was attached to Gage County for judicial purposes. This made it necessary for the sheriff to take them to Beatrice, where they had a preliminary trial before T. M. Coulter, justice of the peace. Hickok rode to Marysville, Kansas, and employed Brumbaugh & Bolinger, attorneys, to defend him. No motive for the crime was shown, so it remained a matter of self-defense. The accused contended they were defending Government property; that is, wagons, horses, stages, and other appliances used in carrying the mails of the United States, and that they were defending their own lives and the lives of others. Monroe McCanles was summoned as a witness but was not placed on the stand of prosecution, which had already collapsed before the trial. Public sentiment had acquitted the defendants, and witnesses could do the prosecution no good. The accused men were not held for trial in a higher court.

Wild Bill and McCanles were both men of strength and character. Trouble between men of such types and in such a setting was pretty certain to have its ending only in the death of one or the other. By his courage and skill, his iron will, and his achievements Wild Bill won fame. And by his tragic death undesired notoriety was given to McCanles.

CHAPTER VII · *How Wild Bill Got His Name*

I N 1861 Fort Leavenworth was in the Western Department. It was the depot for military supplies for Kansas and Nebraska, and was drawn upon by the military forces of Missouri. The headquarters of the Department were at St. Louis. The Commandant of Fort Leavenworth in 1861 was Captain W. E. Prince.

When Hickok left Rock Creek Station, he went to Fort Leavenworth. This was before the first of August 1861. He offered his services to contractors for transportation for the Government, and was given charge of a train carrying supplies from Fort Leavenworth to Sedalia, Missouri. Just when Hickok's train left Fort Leavenworth is not known. It was evidently prior to the siege of Lexington by General Price, and must have been prior to August 10, 1861, the date of the battle of Wilson Creek.

On the third day out from Fort Leavenworth, guerrillas attacked the train, not far from Independence. The guard, consisting of twelve men, did not make any serious effort to defend the train, but retreated, in which action it was probably justified, for the guerrilla force consisted of fifty or more men. The train was captured and some of the wagons were burned. Hickok, as master of the train, was not driving a wagon, but was mounted on horseback.

Called upon to surrender, he replied, "Come and take me," and put his horse at full speed on the road toward Independence. He was pursued by part of the guerrillas, all firing

44

at him, but he escaped without a scratch. He fired back on
his pursuers and killed some of them. It was after dark when
Hickok arrived in Independence, which was garrisoned by
Union troops. He stopped to report the loss of the train of
supplies. He was told that no help could be given him at that
point, and that he would have to go on to Kansas City and
report to the Commandant at that post.

Independence was one of the Eastern terminals of the Old
Santa Fé Trail, and in the capacity of wagon-master and
stage-driver Hickok had often been there. He knew many
of the townspeople. Among his acquaintances were the
Youngers, members of the Chiles family, the Walkers, the
Greggs and the Hickmans.

While at Independence Hickok went into a saloon owned
by a friend of his. When he entered, he found a fight had
been in progress for some time, and the bar-tender had taken
sides. He had wounded a man and the assembled mob had
turned against him. He had been chased into a near-by
dwelling where he was surrounded by some fifteen or twenty
teamsters and other rough characters, all demanding that
he come out. Some swore to have his life, and others that he
should be protected.

This was the status of the affair when Hickok arrived. As
soon as he found how matters stood, he drew two pistols and
offered to fight the entire party. This seemed to sober the
besiegers, and none of them manifested any disposition to
accept Hickok's challenge. Finally, Hickok ordered the
crowd to disperse, saying,

"If you do not there will be more dead men around here
than the town can bury." The ruffians departed hurriedly.
It was immediately broadcast through the town that Hickok
had cowed and scattered the band of rowdies who had terrorized the people for some days. He was given a demonstration of approval, and in the crowd were a number of

women. During the meeting, which was on the public square,
some woman cried

"Good for you, Wild Bill."

This name stuck. The crowd took it up, and he was hailed
as Wild Bill. Who this woman was, Hickok never knew, but
the incident gave him the name under which he became
famous.[1]

Hickok went on to Kansas City where he secured a body
of soldiers. He returned to the scene of the attack and succeeded in recapturing the uninjured wagons and some of the
mules of the teams of the wagons which had been burned.
The following day the train was put into condition to proceed. When Hickok arrived at Sedalia, he found that his
fame had preceded him, and he was accosted everywhere
as "Wild Bill."

CHAPTER VIII · *Preliminary Services in Missouri for the Union*

AT THE beginning of the Civil War, the border counties of Missouri contained many rough and turbulent characters. They had been engaged in the commerce of the prairies over the Old Santa Fé Trail. Many of them were Border Ruffians who had invaded Kansas in her territorial days, burned houses, murdered settlers and sacked and plundered towns. Many of the good people of Missouri favored the South in the Civil War, and were moderate in their attitude toward those who stood for the Union. And of those who were loyal to the government there were many in every county. These people organized themselves as best they could, for the general government was slow to come to their aid, and the border of Kansas and Missouri from 1855 to 1856 was the most turbulent in America. Families were divided, communities were torn asunder. Dead men ornamented trees by the roadside, and were found lying in fields and in byways.

Into this seething and contradictory community came Hickok. When Hickok entered the service of transportation for the Government cannot now be definitely fixed, but it must have been two or three weeks prior to the first of August. It is certain that he was in the battle of Wilson Creek. A record of his enlistment in any Missouri regiment has not been found. Hickok seems to have been attached to the headquarters of the officers commanding the forces in the field in Southwest Missouri, Northwest Arkansas, and the Indian Territory and he was detailed for any and every kind of emergency.

John C. McKoin was born at Russellville, Logan County, Kentucky, in 1836, and was brought to Greene County, Missouri, in 1839. He made many trips into the Indian Territory to trade with the Indians. He traveled on trading tours over Northwest Arkansas and Southwest Missouri and became a trader and freighter over the Old Santa Fé Trail. In this business McKoin met Hickok, and their acquaintance ripened into true friendship. Together they rode, drove, suffered from the heat and the cold, fought the Indians, and hunted. When McKoin married Miss Christiana Scott at Spring Hill, Kansas, Hickok was the best man at his wedding. McKoin went to Greene County, Missouri, to live. Hickok, turned toward Missouri by the progress of the Civil War, sought out his old-time friend. The presence of Hickok at Springfield prior to the battle of Wilson Creek was due to this visit to McKoin.[1]

The battle of Wilson Creek was the result of the efforts of General Lyon to establish the Union firmly in authority throughout Missouri. He set out to clear the State of Confederate forces and make Missouri a powerful factor for the Union in the war. Springfield was recognized by him as the vital outpost of St. Louis. General Lyon by the middle of July 1861 was in possession of Springfield and much of Southwest Missouri. General McCulloch, however, was moving up the Wire Road, and General Price coöperated with him against Lyon. There were preliminary battles at Crane Creek, Dug Springs, and McCulla's Store, with the result that by the ninth of August the Confederates were massed at Wilson Creek, ten miles southwest of Springfield, on both sides of the Wire Road. Against his judgment, General Lyon accepted the plan put forward by Colonel Sigel, which was to divide the army and attack from two positions simultaneously.

This was done and proved disastrous to Lyon and Sigel, as it did to Price and McCulloch at Pea Ridge some months later.

The attack was made about daybreak on the tenth of July. Colonel Sigel's division was fairly successful in its attack, until a portion of his battery was lost when he mistook enemy troops for Lyon's men. General Lyon had that section of the Confederate force which he had attacked, in flight down the Wire Road, when he was killed. The fleeing Southerners halted, and turned back. Both Union and Confederate forces claimed the victory. In reality, the battle resulted in neither victory for the Confederates, nor defeat for the Union forces.

Hickok was in this battle. We do not know what part he played. He himself says that he was on the skirmish line; that is, he was in the advance, and in the gravest danger. Acting as a sharpshooter it is probable that he killed many men. In any event, he stood with Lyon's troops and held his ground. In the retreat to Rolla, he was in the rear facing the enemy should an enemy appear.

In October 1861, General Fremont moved against General Price with the object of clearing Missouri of Confederate forces. Price was in retreat, after having taken Lexington, and was moving toward the Arkansas line. On the evening of October 24, General Fremont directed Major Charles Zagonyi, commander of his bodyguard, with 150 men, and Major F. J. White, with 180 men to make a reconnaissance in the direction of Springfield. At noon on October 25, these commands were eight miles north of Springfield. Majors Zagonyi and White decided to attack, even though they knew positively that they were outnumbered by the enemy five to one.

It was late in the afternoon of the twenty-fifth when the Federal forces, emerging from a wood just west of Springfield, came unexpectedly upon the Confederates, formed in line of battle in the west limits of the town. Major Zagonyi was compelled to charge through a long lane, where his troops were under a severe cross-fire. Emerging from this lane, they were thrown into battle-line and ordered to charge. This charge was one of the spectacular movements of the war in Missouri. The troops raised the cry of "Fremont and the Union," and dashed recklessly upon the enemy.

The Confederate line was shattered and the troops dispersed, fleeing through the town. Major Zagonyi assembled his forces in the public square and raised the Union flag over the courthouse. Night was rapidly coming on, and, having suffered heavy loss, Major Zagonyi retired in the direction of the advance of Fremont. In this charge he had lost sixteen men killed, and twenty-six wounded, and he found and buried twenty-three Confederate dead.

Riding by the side of August Jost, a member of Fremont's bodyguard throughout this battle was Hickok. He had been sent to the front with dispatches for Major Zagonyi and arrived as the charge through the lane was ordered. In this charge he killed three men. Jost killed two men, and wounded another. The reckless manner in which Hickok conducted himself in this charge became a matter of comment in the ranks of Federal forces under General Fremont. He delivered his dispatches after the battle.

CHAPTER IX · *Wild Bill's First Scouting Expedition*

ABOUT the first of January 1862, General Curtis, at Rolla, Missouri, who had just assumed his new position as Commander of the Union forces of Southwest Missouri, found it imperative that he have accurate knowledge of the Confederates in that region as well as in Northwest Arkansas. He called for men who knew the country and were familiar with roads, trails, hills, and streams. Among those chosen were John R. Kelso, John C. McKoin, John W. Allen, a squaw-man from the Cherokee Nation, and "Zeke" Stone, also a Cherokee squaw-man. Kelso recommended a young man of great courage who had been in the service a few months—Kelso said he was a fine horseman and a dead shot. His name was J. B. Hickok. So Hickok was added to the scouts. They were directed to ride into the enemy's lines and secure what information they could of Confederate plans. They were to make their own arrangements. They might act together or separately as conditions required. Kelso was placed in charge of them.

They planned to ride east of the general concentration of the Confederate forces to a point south of Fayetteville, and then to follow the Wire Road, as nearly as possible, to Van Buren, Arkansas. This road was the old mail route along which a telegraph wire had been stretched from Rolla, then the end of the railroad from St. Louis, to Van Buren. It passed through Springfield, the Wilson Creek battlefield, by

Elkhorn Tavern to Fayetteville, and then along dividing ridges to Van Buren.

The men knew that their enterprise was a desperate one, and they often separated to ride singly through more dangerous sections. The final assembly was to be at a point about six miles south of Fayetteville. They believed they could go on from there as a party by pretending to be Confederate soldiers on detached service. Hickok became the real leader, though Kelso was in command until the party separated. A jealousy arose between these two men which continued as long as they served together, though there never was an open rupture.

They were in a land of hills and mountains, dense forests and deep, swift, streams. Bands of guerillas and scouting Confederates patroled the roads and trails of this semi-wilderness. Travel by day was often too perilous to be considered and at times it was scarcely less dangerous by night.

Looking as far as he could into the shadows as they advanced one night, Hickok saw something cross the road. The scouts halted. Peering through the dim starlight they thought they could discern mounted men, lurking near a bunch of scrub. So, turning as quietly as possible, they rode behind the turn of a cut-bank in a small stream. Almost at once, men appeared on the bank above them and other men came around the bend in the creek-bed. The scouts drew their pistols, and waited until they were challenged. Their reply to the challenge was five shots which created great confusion among the attackers. The scouts raced up the creek and, coming to a sloping bank, charged up and through their foes, firing and yelling. They were soon clear of their enemies, who seemed content to let them go—from which they reasoned that they must have inflicted some injury. But they knew that the Confederates now held knowledge of their presence in the country and so their danger would be doubled.

They pushed on at such speed as they could make in the darkness. Kelso, riding ahead, discerned more mounted men on a steep hillside. The scouts crossed the creek and dismounted, leaving Allen to hold the horses. They climbed the steep hill to gain the rear of any men hiding there. In a few minutes they could see a squad of mounted men watching the road. The scouts opened fire and the men retreated hastily over the way which the scouts had come. The scouts returned to Allen, mounted and rode back to the highway, which they now believed to be clear. They came shortly into an open valley, down which they traveled until nearly daylight. They then turned into a cedar-brake, where they went into camp, tired and hungry. It was cold, but they dared not build a fire.

At daybreak, they saw a farmhouse in the valley by the side of the road. A woman, emerging from the house, threw fodder over a fence to some cattle and re-entered the house. The watching scouts decided that the chance of obtaining food was worth the risk, and rode to the yard-fence and dismounted. Kelso knocked upon the door. A shot, tearing through the light doorboards and grazing his head, was the answer. At this instant McKoin shouted an alarm, for a number of men were running towards the house from the barn. Also mounted men appeared in the road below the house and the scouts saw themselves trapped. Leaving their mounts, they raced for the rough willow-thicketed bank of the creek back of the house. They fired on the advancing men and Kelso killed one.

In a shower of bullets, the scouts ran down the creek. They were not followed. At the head of a small stream, Kelso stopped to read a paper—for which he had been awaiting sufficient light. He had taken the paper the previous night from the pocket of a coat strapped to the saddle of a dead horse. He did not tell the other men what the paper contained, but stated that he was starting north immediately and taking McKoin along.

He and McKoin started back through the woods at once on foot. That day they ambushed a rebel scouting party and killed three men. They took their horses, two of which they mounted and began to beat down to the west and south. They had many escapes, but finally returned to headquarters, a day or two after the other party got in.

Hickok, Allen, and Stone went on. They bore to the south that day and at nightfall came out on the Wire Road. Allen and Stone said they were five or six miles from Van Buren, and they proceeded in that direction. At a farmhouse near the road they took two hens from a shed. Hickok said he must have a pot in which to cook the chickens, and against the will of the others, he went towards a cabin where he saw a light. No dog barked, and Hickok lifted a kettle from its peg by the door. At the sound, an old negro woman opened the door and peered out. Hickok told her a party of soldiers were up at the big house and some of them wanted to borrow her kettle until morning. He walked off unconcernedly. The men boiled their chickens in a ravine, and then went on to Van Buren, arriving there at daylight.

There were loyal people in Van Buren, some of whom Stone knew. Allen went in search of his Cherokee wife, who was living there with her father's family. She concealed his presence from her people, and gave him all the information she could get—of forces, troops, officers, movements, and supplies. She was three-fourths white and a very intelligent woman.[1]

Hickok always insisted that the success of the expedition was due to the shrewdness of Mrs. Allen. She went with Hickok to Fort Smith, where she introduced him to some Choctaw girls of her acquaintance. Finally Mrs. Allen obtained the specific information which she was seeking for the scouts. On her advice, the scouts prepared to press on. It was long past midnight when they made their start. They searched the roads coming in from the east and finally identified the one to which Mrs. Allen had directed them. It ran through heavy timber. At daylight the scouts concealed themselves in a tangled bunch of bushes and vines. There was a cabin in a field on the south.

Early in the morning a party of six Confederates and one man in civilian dress appeared upon the road, rising toward Van Buren. The scouts had not expected so many and they were in doubt, thinking this might not be the party expected. But seeing the Captain in a blazing new uniform, Hickok said he knew that he was the man for whom Mrs. Allen had told him to watch. The scouts rode into the land and Hickok cried, "halt!" The Captain fired at the scouts, and turning his horse, made for the timber. The others fired and charged, and the scouts began to fire. Hickok killed a man, as did Allen. The remaining Confederates turned and raced after the Captain. The scouts pursued at top speed. Hickok outdistanced his comrades and left them far behind—for the horse he was riding was a very fast one. In a few minutes Stone and Allen passed a dead Confederate lying in the road. In five minutes they came upon another dead Confederate and his wildly excited horse.

Passing the second dead man, Stone and Allen came into the wider clearings, from which the road descended to lower land. Far across a streamless valley they saw Hickok closing in on the Captain and his lone comrade. In a minute Hickok shot the remaining soldier, who fell backward and was dragged by his foot which had caught in the stirrup, and Hickok had some trouble in passing the terror-stricken horse. Allen wondered why he had not killed the Captain in the first place.

Hickok bore rapidly down upon the Captain, who turned

in his saddle and fired back repeatedly. Hickok did not fire. Riding beside him, he seized the Captain by the collar and dragged him from his horse. When Stone and Allen came up Hickok was just removing from his captive's clothing small packets of papers. The last one was ripped from his shirt with a bowie as Stone and Allen rode up. The Captain's clothing was ruthlessly slashed and he stood shivering in the raw wind. When Hickok was satisfied that he had obtained all the papers in the possession of the Captain, he told him to go back and get the dead soldier's overcoat and ride on to Van Buren. The Captain was amazed and wanted to know why he was spared the fate of his comrades. Hickok laughed and said the person informing him of the dispatches had added that their bearer was soon to become a happy bridegroom. The young Confederate, downcast and wretched, said that his bride would probably despise him after the failure on his important mission: and that in any event, disgrace awaited him.

Hickok assured the Captain that he was taking the matter too seriously, and that there was no disgrace in his valliant conduct. As to the prospective bride, Hickok prophesied that she would be so overjoyed at her lover's escape that she would care nothing about dispatches. With this parting word Hickok turned his attention to his own affairs.

Having accomplished the object of the invasion of enemy's country, it devolved upon him to deliver the captured dispatches safely to headquarters at Springfield. The scouts rode north through the woods. Under an overhanging rock they decided to build a fire at nightfall. They had no food for themselves or their horses. The next morning they set out again, slowly and with caution. They worked north, all day, hungry and cold. Toward night they found ungathered corn still in a field and fed their horses. Some pumpkins roasted at their campfire, and parched corn furnished them a meal.

The next day they continued their slow advance and camped in the same comfortless fashion that night.

At daylight, the following morning, the party came upon a cabin in a clearing. A negro was working just outside a shed, under which stood some horses. The scouts seized him. Terror-stricken, he answered their questions, saying that the cabin was occupied by guerrillas, four of whom were then inside, with two women. Leaving the scared negro in charge of the other men, Hickok approached the cabin and pushed open the door. Revolvers drawn, he stepped quickly inside. Two men were lying on blankets before the fire. These men yielded, seeing that resistance meant certain death, and were disarmed. Two beds were each occupied by a guerrilla. These men too Hickok disarmed. The girls, who were cooking breakfast, when Hickok pushed open the door, screamed shrilly at his entrance. He bade them be still saying there was no danger as long as they made no resistance. One of these girls was named Susanna Moore. She seemed much impressed by Hickok's appearance and by his early mastery of the four guerrillas. Just what to do was not clear to the scouts. They did not wish to kill the prisoners and could not take them along. And the presence of the girls complicated the situation.

Even as the scouts consulted, the situation changed. A squad of Confederates rode up to the fence and hallooed, taking every one by surprise. The scouts threw open the door and charged out, shooting. One man fell from his saddle dead, and two more were wounded. The others turned and fled. Hickok shouted to his man to mount and pursue. On a muddy stretch of road, the Confederates, compelled to slow a bit, began to return fire. Hickok was riding ahead, and his horse was killed. As he scrambled to his feet, Susanna Moore, who had been riding after the scouts, dashed up and stopped beside him. She slipped from her horse and thrust the reins

into his hand. He mounted. The scouts charged and cleared
the lane. The Confederates ran out on the Wire Road, rendering further pursuit impossible.

Hickok knew that they must make their escape as quickly
as possible, as the Confederates would soon return with reinforcements. Susanna Moore told the scouts that over the
mountain to the east was a road running in a general north-
easterly direction. The scouts accordingly bore to the east;
coming out on the highlands at the heads of the streams
flowing west and north into White River and those flowing
through the Buffalo and other creeks into lower reaches of
the same river. They rode north and crossed the White
River at a point south of Forsyth, Missouri. They went north
through Taney, Christian, and Greene Counties, and arrived at headquarters about the middle of January 1862,
where Hickok delivered his dispatches.

CHAPTER X · *The Battle of Pea Ridge, or Elkhorn Tavern*

Pea Ridge is in Benton County, Arkansas, some fifteen miles west of Eureka Springs, and three or four miles south of the line between the states of Arkansas and Missouri. Elkhorn Tavern stood at its western base, fronting east on the Wire Road. General Sterling Price, in command of the Missouri Confederate troops, evacuated Springfield, February 12, 1862, and General Curtis occupied it the following day. The retreat of General Price was south over the Wire Road, and he was closely pursued by the Union forces, barely escaping with his trains and losing many men. He halted finally at the head of Cove Creek, five or six miles south of Prairie Grove and as far west of the Wire Road. General Curtis was occupying Cross Hollow, a narrow gorge on the Wire Road, from which he had routed the Confederates. From there he sent out detachments to take possession of Fayetteville and other points in Northwest Arkansas.

General Van Dorn, ordered by the authorities at Richmond to assume command of the Confederate forces in Western Arkansas, arrived at Price's headquarters on March 3. He about-faced the Confederates, marching north through Prairie Grove and Rhea's Mills, upon Bentonville. General Curtis, preparing for the inevitable encounter, concentrated his troops at and about Elkhorn Tavern. There and on Pea Ridge was fought a desperate and decisive battle, on the seventh and eighth of March. The Confederates were defeated, and retreated from Northwest Arkansas.

59

In all the advances of General Curtis against the enemy and in the battle of Pea Ridge, Hickok bore a very active part. He was constantly scouting far out in advance of the Union troops. In war, as fought in the days of 1861 to 1865, the scouts were the eyes and ears of the armies. Through them the commanders gained knowledge of the conditions and intentions of their opponents, for a good scout was often required to enter the enemy lines and become spy as well as scout. Only a few of the daring actions of Hickok in those stirring days came to the notice of any except the officers in command. He said nothing about them himself, but he had as a comrade one who greatly admired him, who often rode by his side, and as often faced death with him. In after years this comrade would tell of the awful risks taken and of the narrow escapes. In many instances these accounts were verified by other soldiers, some of high rank.

When the Confederates were at the Wilson Creek battle-field on their retreat from Springfield, Kelso, Allen, Hickok, Stone, McKoin, and a man named Adkins, together with others, were directed to keep in touch with Price's command and report every day. They left Springfield late at night on the fourteenth of February on the Neosho and Springfield road. At daylight on the morning of the fifteenth, they were twenty-five miles out, and they turned south and rode into the lines of Price's retreating army. They were dressed as Confederate soldiers, and Hickok posed as a Confederate Captain. About ten o'clock they encountered a foraging party with ten wagons, the guard consisting of twelve men. The scouts hailed this party and became a part of it. They marched up a narrow valley of a prong of Flat Creek. Soon they came upon a farm with stacks of grain and hay and well-filled corncribs. Six of the wagons were loaded with corn and others were filled with oats and hay. Several hogs, together with turkeys and chickens, were thrown in. The captain of the guard ordered dinner prepared for himself and the men.

At the house the scouts learned that the farm belonged to a widow whose husband had been killed some months before by guerrillas on account of his sympathies for the Union. The widow and her five daughters had tended the crops and reaped the harvest. These women were in despair over the ruin which had overtaken them, and they implored the guard to unload the wagons and leave them what they had worked so hard to raise. To carry it away meant starvation for them.

As Hickok rose from the table after finishing his dinner, he saw some of the teamsters upsetting bee-gums and destroying bees to get the honey. He turned to the Confederate Captain and made an appeal for the women. He said that the glorious Confederacy which he served should not be established on the robbery of women. That he was for unloading the wagons and going in search of some farm where there were men to work. The Confederate Captain opposed that action, saying that the army must be fed. Hickok called for a vote, and only the Captain and three or four men voted to take the hay and grain. In the end they acquiesced in the decision of the majority and the wagons were unloaded.

It was three o'clock when the party retraced its course down the creek. About dark a farm was found from which the family had fled, and here the wagons were filled with whatever could be found. Long after dark the party reached the Wire Road and found hundreds of camp-fires burning. Confusion prevailed. Trains were rolling southward. Regiments of troops were pressing these wagon-trains, and often trying to pass them.

In the darkness and confusion the scouts found it an easy matter to pass for Confederate soldiers. They were unnoticed and they went freely about the camps. Everything which could be learned was in their possession by midnight and Adkins was sent back with it to the Union lines. The

others went into camp with Missourians from Randolph
County, and slept until called by the bugles of the morning.
Most of the army had passed in the night, or at least they
saw only companies and squads on the road as the day
broke over the hills. Those in camp were soon in motion and
the scouts rode with them down the Wire Road toward Elkhorn Tavern.

About three o'clock in the afternoon, the scouts rode
slowly south on the Keetsville and Bentonville Road, which
was off the main line of retreat. Soon after crossing the state
line they met a party of about fifteen Confederates. Apparently one of them recognized Hickok as an enemy, for
the Confederates attacked. The scouts succeeded in killing
three men, and then turned their horses and fled. The Confederates followed, firing as they rode. They were gaining
rapidly on the scouts, and so, at Hickok's direction, the men
left the road and rode behind some scrub bushes at its side.
When the pursuers came even with them, the scouts burst
from hiding and attacked. They killed four of the enemy and
then broke into top speed in pursuit of those who were in
flight. McKoin fired at long range and killed a man, and in a
moment Allen killed another. As Hickok fired, a guerrilla
horse running wild with fright, collided with his horse, and
Hickok and both horses were thrown. Hickok was not injured, but his horse was lame when he got him up.

The men took stock of the situation. Hickok had a lame
horse and was bruised and sore from his fall. There were bul-
let-holes in his clothes, but he had not been wounded. Mc-
Koin found a bullet in his horse's right shoulder and another
in the left hind-quarter. Allen had a wound in the left fore-
arm, but, as his horse was not hit, he was sent back with the
message. The others of the party rode into a camp of Confederate troops and dismounted. They told a story of desperate fighting to protect the rear. All were worn out and soon

after dark the scouts and two of their soldier hosts went to sleep in some wagons. At daylight they were on the march. Soon they spied a number of horses and mules being driven into a field just off the road. All went over to try to get mounts. Hickok selected a fine horse which he pretended was his and began to berate the guards for taking his horse. One of the Confederates soon found a horse, which he took, cursing the guards for horsethieves.

They now moved south with the retreating army, but kept far out on the right wing where they hoped to find Adkins coming into the lines. Shortly after noon, Adkins did arrive. But he came top speed, pursued by a squad of the enemy from whom he had escaped three or four miles back. The scouts hailed him and he was glad to find them there, for the pursuers were gaining. He about-faced and the scouts fired upon the Confederates as they came on a dead run into the lower road, killing one, staggering the pursuit and turning it into a mad scramble for escape. In a chase of three miles the Confederates were dispersed—three killed.

Wild Bill feared they were being compelled to fight more frequently than they should and that they would become too well known to be able to conceal their identity. Safety lay in change of position; accordingly they decided to ride to the extreme advance of the Confederate army. That night they fell in with troops from North Missouri camped near Elkhorn Tavern. Then, avoiding roads, they traveled in the direction of Bentonville, arriving there early in the morning.

From Bentonville the scouts covered the country in front of the Confederate army as far South as Fayetteville. They moved cautiously and were fortunate in avoiding clashes with parties of the enemy. They were several days riding over the counties of Benton and Washington studying the directions and junctions of the roads, especially the obscure and little used cross roads. This gave them a knowledge of the country which was particularly valuable to General Curtis when he arrived at Elkhorn Tavern.

On the fourth of March, Hickok, McKoin, and Allen were scouting south of Rhea's Mills. Advance parties of Confederates bearing north began to appear on all roads. At first they were small, but as the day wore on they become larger, sometimes consisting of as many as twenty men. Sometimes the scouts would fall in and ride with one of these parties. That night Allen rode to the headquarters of General Curtis, while Hickok and McKoin camped with a squad of Texas troops. On the morning of the fifth the scouts hung along the roads and kept under cover as much as possible. The full tide of the Confederate advance could be felt even then, and by noon men were to be seen moving north on all the roads in ever-increasing numbers. Late in the day they were found and joined by Allen and the three of them camped that night with Louisiana troops. The next morning they took to the brush and observed the coming of the Confederates. There were columns and trains and artillery and they knew that a battle was imminent. In the afternoon they were not far south of the Bentonville and Pea Ridge Road.

On the road they met a party of seven Confederates. A running battle resulted in the death of several of the Confederates, and a very slight flesh-wound in the calf of the leg for Hickok. A search of the clothing of the dead leader yielded a number of dispatches. By this time, the scouts could see the smoke of battle, and it was not long until they were in the hearing of guns. Riding far to the east they passed around the Confederate lines, and ran into the Union ranks. The scouts reported to General Curtis, who retained them for service from his headquarters.

During the battle of Pea Ridge, Hickok rode from Headquarters to every part of the field with orders. He changed

horses four times the first day, having exhausted three and
having one shot from under him. The night of the seventh he
did not sleep, but was riding on the skirts of both armies.

On the eighth of March he saw a band of sharpshooters
going to take a position far out to the front, and he requested
permission of General Curtis to join it for a time. He was allowed to go, and he killed several officers and men, but how
many neither he nor any one else ever knew. He did not kill
General McCulloch.[1]

The battle of Elkhorn Tavern was really won by the
Union forces on the first day, the seventh. The battle on the
eighth was fought on the Confederate side without hope.
Late on that day, they were withdrawn by way of an obscure
ravine in the direction of Huntsville. The retreat was so
sudden that Albert Pike was not notified in time to lead his
murderous Indians from the field. He afterward claimed that
he did not retreat at all, but only "left the enemy behind by
rapid riding." He left his plundering Choctaws to escape as
best they could. Many of them did not escape.

The victory of General Curtis settled the fate of Missouri
in the Civil War. The great state was henceforth Northern
territory, a part of the Union, and completely lost to the
South.

* * * * *

Seven guerrillas were detailed to ambush Hickok once as
he was going from Carthage to Springfield. They disguised
themselves as farmers and cut down a tree beside the road
and were splitting it into fence rails. It was their intention
to kill Hickok as he rode by. Hickok entered the timber in
the creek bottom and the ambushers did not see him again
until he had shot two of them dead from a position in their
rear. The others fired hasty shots and ran, but Hickok killed
three of them; the other two escaped into the brush and
saved their lives.

CHAPTER XI · *War-time Adventures of Wild Bill*

I N THE summer of 1861, Wild Bill was given the territory about Yellville, Arkansas, as a field of operations inside the Confederate lines. The weight of the evidence would make his arrival there early in 1861. One statement says that Wild Bill remained at Yellville continuously for eighteen months, but that is improbable. He was there five or six months, however. It is known that he lodged and boarded in the family of a Mr. Estes in the latter part of 1863, so he must have been at Yellville at different times. He was a favorite with the people of Yellville, and Mrs. Estes said that he was "as nice a man at her home as she ever had about her house." While stationed at Yellville Hickok had many narrow escapes and amazing adventures.

From Clarendon, Arkansas, General Curtis sent Wild Bill into the rebel lines. He was to attach himself to the Confederate forces operating along the Arkansas River below Little Rock and to keep General Curtis informed as to the plans and movements of the Confederates.

The Confederate forces were at that time making an effort to capture Devall Bluff. Wild Bill covered the whole territory between Little Rock and the Mississippi River south of the Bluff, and sent General Curtis accounts of what he was seeing and hearing. It was necessary for Bill to work rapidly, as both armies were constantly on the march, and there were many skirmishes. He had been with the Confederates almost two weeks when he was one day recognized by a corporal of a company under the command of Marmaduke, and arrested. A drumhead court-martial was immediately organized. In an hour after his arrest he was sentenced to be shot the following morning at sunrise. The court-martial finished its session about ten o'clock at night, and Bill was taken to a small log cabin where he was to be guarded during the night.

The guard at this cabin consisted of six men, some one of whom was constantly on duty. The door had a sort of home-made lock which, from the inside, was opened with a case-knife. Soon after midnight, a terrific storm rose. There was a strong wind, much thunder and lightning, and rain falling in sheets. Bill sat where he could plainly be seen and pretended to be asleep. But at every flash of lightning he scanned the cabin in search of some means of escape. Finally a flash of lightning revealed to him this old case-knife used to unlock the door. It was in an augur-hole in one of the logs, and the handle only protruded. Moving very cautiously, he raised himself up and secured the knife which he carried as rapidly as he could move without exciting suspicion to a corner of the cabin. Fastening the handle of the knife in a crevice between two logs, he sawed the rope, which held his wrists, across the edge in an effort to cut himself loose. The knife was so dull that many precious moments were lost before the rope was sufficiently weakened to snap under his straining. Cautiously he whetted the knife against his boot sole until its edge was much sharpened. Finally he approached the door and spoke to the guard. He made some trivial request which the man must come inside to grant. As he stepped in, Bill seized him by the hair with the left hand and cut his throat with the old case-knife in his right hand. His action was as quick as the lightning which was still flashing.

Surveying the surroundings through the cracks between

the logs of the cabin, Bill saw the other members of the guard
under a small shed some thirty or forty feet away. He
stripped the dead guard and put on his clothes. Then taking
up the musket which the guard had dropped, he stepped outside and remained at the sentinel's place, waiting for an opportunity to slip into the brush. Very soon he was going
through a cane-brake in the storm. He went north to where
he believed he would find General Curtis, but found only the
trail where the army had passed. This he followed to the east
and south, keeping under cover, and reached the army late
in the evening of the following day. He always insisted that
this was one of the closest places he was ever in during his
entire service of scouting.

In the month of November 1861, the Confederate forces
at Yellville amounted to about one thousand men, commanded by Colonel Burbridge. Large saltpeter works were
erected there. Lead was mined in the vicinity, powder was
made there, and ammunition was manufactured. An arsenal
of no mean proportions resulted from the activities of the
Confederates. Wild Bill kept General Curtis informed of
what was being done there.

At the direction of General Curtis, Colonel Wickersham
marched day and night over a rough country and reaching
Yellville, attacked the Confederate forces and drove them
from the town. He destroyed the saltpeter works, burned the
arsenal and storehouses, and destroyed five hundred rifles
and shotguns which he found there, and captured one
hundred horses. The Confederate forces were scattered and
made no attempt to reëstablish themselves at Yellville.

In the Helena campaign, Wild Bill had met a Confederate
soldier named Jake Lawson, and they had become friends.
Wild Bill soon recognized Lawson at Yellville, and was fearful that Lawson would recognize him. He knew that if he
was suspected and arrested the second time as a spy in the

Confederate lines he would be summarily shot, and he determined to escape at the crossing of White River. When the opposing forces were drawn up on the banks of the River, Bill challenged Lawson to ride as near the Union line as possible. He proposed that they ride along at the edge of the water in front of their camp on the south side of the river, saying that the Union forces should be shown a little Southern gallantry and bravado. Lawson was reluctant and called the plan foolhardy. But being taunted by his comrades, he acquiesced. He and Bill mounted their horses and dashed toward the river, riding some distance apart. The Union troops, not understanding, began to fire on Bill and Lawson. The fire became so hot that Bill called across the river, saying, "Hold your fire! I am Wild Bill trying to get into the lines." Hearing this and seeing the trick, Lawson attempted to kill him, but before he could draw a gun Bill had sent a bullet through his brain. He seized the bridle of the dead man's horse, and dashed into the river. The Confederates fired at Bill as he swam. Bullets fell thick as hail around him, but he was not hit. He emerged from the river among Union troops where his information as to the condition at Yellville was of the first importance.

In the fall of 1863 Wild Bill was sent with dispatches from Springfield to Rolla. About twenty miles out from Rolla he saw three guerrillas ride into the road from a cross-trail some distance ahead. They were well mounted, and, having decided to kill or capture them, he pressed forward to overtake them. He was soon able to dispatch two of the men, but the third, a very large heavy man, carrying a bundle, was mounted on a magnificent black steed. This horse, in spite of the weight of its rider, fairly flew over the ground. The chase was a long and hard one, with Bill urging his mount on, relentlessly. Finally the chase headed down a steep hill. At a fork of the road the guerrilla turned to the

right. Bill saw the guerrilla going down, and he had reduced
his speed. It was plain that the guerrilla would escape if
Bill followed the road in pursuit. He jumped from his horse
and ran down the hill toward the turn the guerrilla would
have to make at the foot of the slope. He arrived there in
time to face the guerrilla, who instantly fired at him, the
ball going through his hat. Bill fired and the guerrilla struck
the road dead. On examination, the bundle he carried proved
to be about a bushel of Confederate paper money to pay off
a bunch of guerrillas, the roll of which was found in the bag.

The horse, released of its burden, bounded lightly back
up the hill. Bill followed, and the horse finally came to a stop
by a fence at the top of the hill. It stood, tossing its head a
moment, then turned to look at Bill who was coming up
slowly. He saw it was a mare—he thought the finest he had
ever seen. She seemed perfect, and after her terrific exertion,
was not blown nor exhausted. Bill mounted her and then
knew he had captured a prize beyond price. He rounded up
the other horses and drove them into Rolla. The mare, having been captured, belonged to the Government. Bill had the
quartermaster appraise her and he paid down the $225.00
fixed as her value, and took her. He named her Nell. Under
his care and training she became the wonder of the army in
Missouri.[1]

Late in the fall of 1863, Wild Bill was requested to enter
the Confederate lines in Texas, Louisiana, and South Arkansas, and to remain there until the plans for the spring movements of troops were duly matured. This was to be a pro-
longed, delicate, and very dangerous undertaking, and Bill
believed that he could accomplish his purpose better if he
had someone with him. This permission was |granted him,
and he chose Allen, who had been his companion on so many
of his scouting expeditions, who had faced death with him
a hundred times. They first rode to Council Grove. From

that point they worked their way south to Dallas, Texas. From Dallas, they rode to a point near Texarkana, where they reported themselves as contractors to deliver cattle to the army. Leaving Texarkana, they rode into the thinly settled part of Arkansas, and stopped just beyond Red River. Here they separated to disguise themselves, and to meet as strangers at Camden, where they would make application for enlistment in the Confederate army.

Bill purchased a ragged and patched suit of clothes from an old farmer, and traded his horse for an old Jack belonging to the same farmer. Allen followed the same procedure. Thus dressed and equipped, they met at Camden and rode together to Confederate headquarters. The glorious army of the South was to receive two new recruits.

The droll answers of these raw recruits from the back-settlements to the local recruiting officer kept the crowd lounging about the headquarters roaring with laughter. They were accepted, and given uniforms and better mounts. They gradually came to a better understanding of things, and learned the ways of soldiering rapidly. By claiming familiarity with the country along the Choctaw line, they were sent into that region with scouting parties. On one of these expeditions they were in the vicinity of Fort Smith, which was then occupied by Union soldiers. Bill was permitted to enter the town one night, and returning to camp with a great quantity of useless information, and riding Black Nell which he had left at that point. They remained with the Confederates until the expedition, under General Steele, reached Prairie d'Ane.

On the night of April 11, they determined to leave the rebels and run into the Union lines as soon as possible. The cavalry divisions of General Price's army were the only Confederate troops engaged in the battle of Prairie d'Ane. No opportunity presented itself for the escape of the Union spies, and they decided to make a bold dash if the Federal lines approached the rebel lines on the twelfth. About noon on the twelfth, General Steele moved forward with his whole force and went into battle-formation near the center of the Prairie. He stood there in battle array for six hours and did nothing except occasionally fire on the enemy with his artillery.

About four o'clock, two men were observed riding out of the rebel lines toward the Union lines. They rode swiftly and were pursued by two Confederate officers and some soldiers, who commanded them to halt, and to whom they paid no attention. The men in the Union ranks at first believed the two men in advance to be rebel scouts, and they were confirmed in this belief a little later, for they turned and rode back toward the rebel lines, almost meeting their pursuers. The officers were almost on them and firing at them. The The Federal soldiers saw the horses of the fugitives rise in the air for a mightly leap, and they saw one man fall from his horse—shot dead. The man who was unhurt turned while his horse was in the air and fired back, killing both officers. When the horses had cleared the obstruction they continued at terriffic speed to approach the Federal lines. Before the survivor reached the line he was recognized and acclaimed "Wild Bill." He was riding Black Nell.

A shout of triumph from the ten thousand troops in line greeted him, and he was the hero of the day. The man who was killed was Allen. Bill did not receive a scratch.[2]

The Confederates were only bluffing at Prairie d'Ane, and when Wild Bill escaped and was seen to go into the Federal lines the rebel troops disappeared from the field and the battle was over.

Frank M. Stahl is an old soldier living in Auburn, Shawnee County, Kansas. He came into the rooms of the Kansas State Historical Society in 1926. Asked if he knew Wild Bill, he said that he did know him, that he saw him in the Civil War at Springfield, Missouri, and at Dardanelle and Little Rock, Arkansas, and was well acquainted with him. At Dardanelle, Stahl was badly wounded. Wild Bill found him lying on a pile of corn cobs in some stable or crib. Bill looked at him and thought he could not live, so he said to him, "Frank, I am going to fix you so you will die easy." He then arranged Stahl in a comfortable position, and put a blanket under his head. Stahl was not so badly wounded as they supposed, and he recovered.

After General Steele returned to Little Rock from the Camden expedition, Stahl was in that city. A disturbance arose one night in the camp between a number of soldiers. In settling it, and trying to prevent the soldiers from killing one another, Hickok was shot in the right side in the abdomen, and Stahl saw him carried into a hospital. In a few days, Stahl was detailed with others to ride from Little Rock to Fort Smith. They had been two days on the road when they were overtaken by a steamboat. The boat landed opposite them, and a number of Union soldiers disembarked, among them Wild Bill. He seemed none the worse for his wound, and took up his duties as though nothing had happened, although Stahl knows that it was a serious wound.

CHAPTER XII · *Girls in a Death Grapple*

DAVE TUTT was not the only Confederate deserter in Arkansas who turned Federal scout and spy. There were many others. Mountaineers are of independent character, and sometimes there was one who could not take the orders with good grace. Strict military usage did not accord with his ideas of the dignity of a free American citizen or soldier. There was nothing of cowardice in his attitude or even hesitancy to battle to the death, but when assigned to a menial task, he revolted.

All of this was exemplified in the conduct of a young man named Gordon. He was born at Charleston, Arkansas, and during the first part of the war, proved to be a splendid Confederate soldier. His immediate grievance was the refusal of a furlough to visit his home while in command of a company in service east of the Mississippi. This was the consummation of a list of supposed indignities. He deserted and returned home. Efforts to arrest him were unavailing and served to drive him into the Federal service, a unit of which he organized along sanguinary and vengeful lines. Confederates along the river below Fort Smith soon felt the weight of his hand. In 1864 he expanded his operations to include a large territory north of the Arkansas river. From the rugged Boston Hills he descended upon couriers of the Confederates rendering communication between Little Rock and the Upper Country very dangerous and difficult.

General Shelby was ordered to suppress Gordon, which task he in turn transmitted to Colonel John T. Crisp. Crisp

selected Captain William H. Gregg for the tough job which
had fallen to his command. Captain Gregg, with fifty men,
scoured the regions about Van Buren and Ozark and penetrated the hills far to the north of these points, but finally
returned to Dardanelle without having sighted Gordon.

The foray of Gregg having failed, the operations of Gordon became ever more daring. The demands for his suppres-
sion increased. Finally, a woman proved to be his Nemesis.
Agnes Masterson was the daughter of a farmer living north
of Ozark. She had been engaged to be married to a young
Confederate soldier who lived on a neighboring farm. He
had been wounded, and had returned home to recover. His
home then became the rendezvous of guerrillas, and one
night it was attacked by Gordon. The young Confederate
was killed. Agnes Masterson was furious and her wrath was
poured out on the commanders of Confederate posts along
the Arkansas. Her rage broke before Gregg departed, and
when he returned empty-handed her fury knew no bounds.
The Mastersons had been loyal to the Union, and one of
the sons was a member of Gordon's band. After the murder
of his sister's lover, he deserted Gordon and joined the Confederate army. From him she secured information as to the
location of Gordon's quarters and the trails leading to his
camps.

Crisp commanded the second expedition of one hundred
or more men detailed to capture Gordon. Agnes Masterson,
having information as to routes and localities, accompanied
him as guide. Gordon had erected for shelter and defense
some log cabins in the Boston Mountains near the southwest corner of the present Searcy County. It required three
days for Crisp's cavalcade to reach this fortification. In its
near vicinity, Crisp was informed by a settler that Gordon
was then in his fort with about forty men. It was determined
to attack at daylight, the next morning.

Early in the engagement Gordon was killed. His men,
being outnumbered more than three to one, retreated and
many of them were killed. Agnes Masterson had Gordon's
body carried into the building of the fort. What indignities
she heaped on the body of the dead soldier are not known,
but she was seen to kick the corpse. His friends found him
mutilated and scalped. Friends of Agnes Masterson denied
later that she had done this. Whoops and exultations re-
sounded among the hills. Whiskey was found in Gordon's
fortress and this the Confederates drank. It was with difficulty that Crisp got his force into marching order. Agnes
Masterson was the last to mount her horse. The loot of the
fort encumbered the Confederates, and the column descended to the valley with difficulty.

The parents of Susanna Moore then lived five or six miles
from Gordon's Fort. Wild Bill with a guard of ten men had
been sent into that region to make observations and he had
stopped that night at her home. Some of Gordon's fleeing
men arrived at the Moore home shortly after daylight and
reported the battle at Gordon's Fort. Gordon and Wild Bill
had been friends. Bill called his men to mount. They made
off at top-speed for the field of action. Susanna Moore rode
at his side. Ordered by him to return, she refused. Bill struck
the rebel line just as it was getting under way. The surprise
was complete. He charged through the Confederates, leaving
twenty or more dead and losing four men himself. He entered the fort and prepared for battle. The Confederates had
little stomach for more fighting, but Crisp pushed them up
again.

Agnes Masterson was furious and challenged Susanna,
whom she knew well, to come out and meet her single-
handed. Before Bill could stop her Susanna had opened the
gate and ridden out. Both girls fired as Susanna advanced.
She came on full tilt, striking Agnes Masterson's horse and

throwing horse and rider over the embankment of the road. She forced her horse down over the bank and the impact of meeting threw both horses. The girls were dismounted. Their pistols were shot out, but they grappled with determination each to kill the other. They fought fiercely as tigers. They fell and rolled down the mountain, locked together, striking and screaming. Just below them was an abrupt ledge of rock forming a cliff of some considerable height. On the brink of this cliff Susanna struck the Masterson girl in the face breaking her hold, and threw her over. Miss Masterson, terrified, screamed as she fell from bush to bush. She landed finally in the top of a cedar-tree. Confederate soldiers, attracted by the cries of the girls, hurried back. Seeing Agnes Masterson thrown over the cliff they fired at Susanna.

Wild Bill reached her at this instant and forcibly dragged her back into the fort, after having killed two of the rebels. The others fled taking with them the Masterson girl. Neither girl was subdued; both would have continued the fight.

The battle raged for two hours, but the Confederates could not recapture the fort. The defenders were reduced to nine men and Susanna, who proved one of the most savage and reckless fighters on the Union side. The Confederates retreated at last, having lost thirty or more men in their assault.

CHAPTER XIII · *The Price Raid of 1864*

THE Price raid into Missouri occurred in 1864. It was organized primarily for loot and robbery, and was started upon with the full knowledge that, though it proved successful, it could not help the Trans-Mississippi department.

General Price crossed the Arkansas River at Dardanelle, September 7, 1864. He crossed through North Central Arkansas into Missouri and drove General Ewing from Pilot Knob on the twenty-sixth. He passed around Jefferson City, as it was too well fortified to meet his taste. On September 8, General Pleasanton arrived in Jefferson City and assumed command of all the Union troops then involved in the movement against Price. He organized the forces at his disposal in a way to inflict the greatest damage on Price's army, and immediately took the pursuit. In the meantime, General Curtis, who had been conducting a campaign against the Indians in Kansas and to the westward, began to assemble an army to oppose Price along the border. General Blunt stood across Price's path at Lexington. General Curtis had ordered out the Kansas militia, and some twenty thousand men responded. He put the State of Kansas under martial law.

Price had crossed the Little Blue. He was ready to destroy Kansas City and invade Kansas. General Pleasanton was closing in on his rear, and there had been constant fighting from Lexington to Kansas City. General Curtis concentrated his army on the prairie south of Westport, and on October 23, General Price was badly defeated and forced to turn south and run for his life. He had anticipated defeat. His train of loot was the longest ever gathered by an army in America. He had miles and miles of wagons laden with plunder of every description—plows, hoes, harrows, furniture, bedding, household goods, clothing torn from the bodies of women and children. During the battle of Westport, this train was moving steadily southward and Price succeeded in salvaging the loot.

Wild Bill, who had been in the service of General Pleasanton, was again requested to enter the Confederate lines as a spy. He did so just before the rebels crossed the state line into Missouri. "Zeke" Stone accompanied him. But it was impossible for Wild Bill to remain long with safety in the Confederate lines. He was too well known. A few days later, when the lines for a battle were being formed, two horsemen were seen to leave the Confederate lines and ride full speed to the Union lines. For audacity, this was one of the boldest escapes made by Wild Bill during the Civil War. The whole rebel command fired at him, and his companion Stone was killed. When the survivor approached the Union line, he was recognized by a friend, who shouted, "It's Wild Bill, the Union Scout." Then a cheer greeted Hickok, who brought information that was of the first importance.

Hickok rode with the Union scouts, and was at the battles of Little Blue, October 21, 1864; Big Blue, October 22, 1864; and Westport, October 23, 1864. Just before the battle of Westport, Wild Bill met his old friend, General Curtis, who was in command of the troops at Kansas City to oppose Price, and as soon as General Pleasanton could be consulted he was transferred from scout duty for Pleasanton to scout for General Curtis, and was with the Union troops in the pursuit of Price.

In Bates County, Missouri, Wild Bill found a squad of Confederates robbing a house. The household goods had all been placed in the farm wagon. Bill was alone, but there were numbers of Union scouts swarming on the heels of the retreating Confederates. He felt that he might take a chance on some of them coming up in time to assist him if he attacked these robbers, so he rode down on them, and before they were aware of his presence he had shot three men. Three others ran into the house and barricaded the door. There was nothing for Bill to do but look for help. Riding back a mile, he saw a command going across country at full speed, and he hailed it. But they were unable to give him aid; accordingly, alone, he went back to the house, which he found in flames. The three soldiers, who had decided to abandon their wagon and team and save themselves, were just mounting their horses when Bill came in sight. They ran south toward the rebel lines. When Bill came within range, the rebels turned in their saddles and fired at him. He killed one of these guerrillas by a long shot. He closed in on the other two, and shot one of them. At this instant, a man in the Union uniform appeared, running for life and pursued by three or four rebels. Bill disposed of the last of those he was chasing, and went to the aid of the fleeing soldier. The Confederates were firing at the fugitive. Bill rode up and found that it was his old friend, Theodore Bartles, one of the original band of Red Legs. They turned about and charged the pursuing Confederates and killed them all, although the pursuit covered three or four miles.

In the Cherokee Nation, Wild Bill was riding along a bridle-path from one command of the Union troops to another, bearing orders. Late in the afternoon he saw three horsemen ahead who halted at sight of him. He opened fire on the three, and killed two of them outright. The other fled. Bill pursued him. Within half a mile he ran into an ambush of fifteen men and was captured. The Confederates told him they were taking no prisoners. It was a wet, cold day, and

the guerrillas decided to go into camp in a cabin which could
be seen in a patch of clearing. Bill's execution was post-
poned until they reached this cabin, when he was to be questioned before his death. They were dismounting in the yard
of the cabin when the door was thrown open and Union
scouts emerged, firing as they came out. The Confederates
took to their heels and disappeared, leaving four dead and
one wounded. Commanding this scout was Al. Saviers, and
Theodore Bartles was one of the company. It was a band of
Red Legs.

CHAPTER XIV · *The Killing of Dave Tutt*

IN 1865, Springfield, Missouri, contained many rough characters. All were armed. Their dress was half that of the frontiersman, half that of the Union soldier. Some were garbed in leather, soiled and black from the grease of campfire cookery. In Springfield there were no paved streets and but few sidewalks. Livestock roamed the streets, and hogs wallowed in mud-holes in the Public Square. The Public Square is unlike that of any other town or city. It contains about three acres of land. Four streets enter this square: St. Louis Street from the east, College Street from the west, Boonville Street from the north, South Street from the south. These streets enter from the middle of each side of the square, and if extended they would cross in the center of the square. This square is the heart of what was formerly known as Old Town, the original Springfield. During the Civil War, it was the business part of the city, and even now the big business houses are grouped around it. At the close of the war Springfield contained about three thousand people.

Dave Tutt was born at Yellville, Arkansas. His father was killed in the Tutt-Everett feud, which raged in Marion County, Arkansas, before the Civil War, and in which forty-five men lost their lives. The Tutt home was a log cabin on Crooked Creek. The cabin is known as "Tutt's Cabin," and it was built by Dave Tutt's father. In the year 1900 the "Widow Tutt," mother of Dave Tutt, was living in this cabin. There were two sons and a daughter, said to have been a very beautiful girl. While Wild Bill was stationed at

Yellville he is said to have had an affair with Miss Tutt. This has been denied, but at least they were close friends.

Tutt was a soldier in the Confederate army. He went with General Curtis, in the spring of 1862, as he passed through Yellville on his way to the Missouri River. Tutt seems to have gone to Springfield, Missouri, and he and Hickok returned from Springfield to Yellville together. Tutt bore a good reputation at Yellville, except that he was a professional gambler. Tutt brought his mother and her family to Springfield in the spring of 1865. Some authorities claim that he was not an expert shot with the pistol; others claim that he was a dead shot.

Wild Bill had been retained as scout as long as troops were in Southwest Missouri, and was in active service in February 1865. After the surrender and the withdrawal of troops from Missouri, Wild Bill remained at Springfield until January 1866. Tutt also remained in Springfield after the surrender. Until within two or three months of the fatal encounter, Tutt and Bill had been friends and companions.

In the first scouting expedition, it will be remembered, Wild Bill had met a girl named Susanna Moore. She came to Springfield in the fall and was with Bill, there, for a time. Whether Bill tired of her, or whether she for a time broke relations with him of her own accord is not known, but she and Tutt became close friends. The appearance of Miss Tutt at Springfield had deeply disturbed Susanna Moore. If there had been an affair between Bill and Tutt's sister it seems not to have been a factor in the antagonism which developed between the two men. The writer never heard it mentioned in Springfield as a cause of bad feeling, although he did hear much of the bad blood which was stirred by the attentions of Tutt to Susanna Moore. That matter must have been what the informant of Mr. Nichols, writer of the *Harper's Magazine* article, meant when he said, "The fact is, there was an under-current of a woman in that fight."

After bad blood developed between Wild Bill and Tutt, Tutt became the aggressive party. He made up his mind to force Bill to a show of resistance, and then kill him. Understanding this, and having no desire for trouble with Tutt, Bill was patient under persistent aggravation. Bill had many enemies at Springfield, as a positive character will have at any place or time. Tutt associated with these enemies of Bill. Bill began to see that soon he would have to act on the defensive.

It came to the point that Bill would not play in any card game where Tutt was a party. Tutt would stand behind anyone playing against Bill, and make suggestions as to the playing of his hand. If the man lost his money Tutt would immediately loan him more money with which to play against Bill. This course was taken to aggravate Wild Bill into an attack. In such a game, on the night of July 20, 1865, Bill won, despite Tutt's coaching of his opponent. This was in a room in the Old Southern Hotel or Lyon House, standing on the east side of South Street, less than a block from the Public Square. During the war it was called the Lyon House in honor of General Lyon. It was still in use as a hotel in the year 1888. But at the time of the tragedy, it was the principal hotel of the town, kept in the way that all hotels were managed on the frontier in the time of the Civil War. The bar was the most imposing feature of the establishment.

On this particular night, though Tutt had loaned Bill's opponent money, Bill had won about two hundred dollars. Tutt was in a fury at the result of the game, and he accosted Bill with, "Bill, you've got plenty of money—pay me that forty dollars you owe me on that horse trade." Bill paid him the forty dollars, and Tutt then said, "You owe me thirty-five dollars more; you lost it playing with me t'other night." Bill answered, "I think you are wrong, Dave. It's only

twenty-five dollars. I have a memorandum of it in my pocket
down-stairs. If it's thirty-five dollars I'll give it to you."
Bill's watch was lying on the table. Tutt picked it up, and
put it in his pocket, saying "I'll keep this watch 'til you pay
me that thirty-five dollars." This angered Bill. But with a
great effort he controlled himself and said quietly, "I don't
want to make a row in this house. But you had better put
that watch back on the table." Dave sneered at Bill, and
walked away with the watch.

Everybody knew Wild Bill's watch, and after it had been
surrendered to Tutt, Bill asked him as an especial favor not
to wear it publicly, or let people know that it had changed
owners. Tutt laughed at Bill and assured him that it would
give him as much pleasure to wear the watch on the streets
as it had already given him to take it. "I intend wearing it in
the morning," Tutt said. Bill replied with an oath, "If you
do, I'll shoot you. I warn you not to come across the square
with it on." Thus the two men parted.

As to when the killing occurred, there is contradiction in
the records. The *Harper's Monthly* account says that Tutt
kept the watch several days, and that the town was full of
talk about the incident. Bill's enemies blackguarded him, and
taunted him in an underhand way in an effort to make him
fight, but they could not provoke Bill into a row. One day
his enemies drew their pistols on him and dared him to fight,
and told him that Tutt was going to pack that watch across
the Square the next day at noon.

Whether or not the killing was on July 21, which was Friday, as stated in the *History of Greene County*, or several days
after the gambling episode, it occurred in this manner: Tutt
passed along the west side of the Square, and entered the
livery stable on the northwest corner. He sat in the door
from which he had a good view of all the four sides of the
Square, and where he could see the Lyon House and far

down South Street. He saw Hickok come out of the hotel and up South Street to the Square. Bill stopped on the west side of the street where he inquired of bystanders if they had seen Dave Tutt down town that morning. They told him that Tutt was on the Square, and Bill said that that was all right if he wasn't wearing his watch, but if he was wearing it "there'll be merry hell, you bet your life."

At this point Tutt's younger brother came up, and Bill said to him that he had better go and tell Dave to take off that watch. Young Tutt replied that Dave had a right to wear the watch. At that moment Tutt came out of the livery stable and walked south along the west side of the square. Bill said, "There he comes now." The idle group of men standing about Bill saw there was likely to be a gun-battle and scattered. But Tutt's friends gathered in a knot and kept close to Bill.

Wild Bill took a few steps forward and drew his revolver, a Colt's Dragoon, a cap-and-ball weapon. When Tutt reached the courthouse, he started east across the Square. Bill called to him and said, "Dave, don't you come across here with that watch." Tutt, about half-way across the Square, but near the north side, drew his pistol and instantly fired. Bill then fired, using his left arm as a rest for his revolver. Tutt was shot through the heart, and died soon. At the trial witnesses said that Tutt's revolver was out of its scabbard when the body was first examined, and that Tutt had fired first. It is certain that one chamber of the revolver was empty, and some of the witnesses testified that they heard two shots. It was acknowledged that Bill's shot was a remarkable one. Bill shot seventy-five yards at Tutt.

In the *History of Greene County* there is no mention of Bill's turning to Tutt's friends immediately after firing and asking them if they were satisfied. In the *Harper's Magazine* article it is said that the instant Bill fired he wheeled, with-

out waiting to see if he hit Tutt, and pointed his pistol at
Tutt's friends who had already drawn their weapons. "Aren't
you satisfied, gentlemen," cried Bill, as cool as an alligator.
"Put up your shootin' arms, or there'll be more dead men
here," and they put them up, and said that it was a fair
fight. The same account says, "Bill never shoots twice at the
same man, and his ball went through Dave's heart. He
(Dave) stood stock still for a second or two, then raised his
arm as if to fire again; then swayed a little, staggered three
or four steps, and fell dead."

Robert McClary was a soldier at Springfield at the time
that Tutt was killed. He is now an inmate of the National
Soldiers Home for Kansas. He states that he was standing on
the north side of the Square, and saw Tutt on the west side
in front of Young's livery stable. He saw Wild Bill come on
the Square from South Street. There were some ox-teams
standing in the Square which cut off his view when Wild Bill
first entered the Square. Tutt ran about thirty steps out on
the Square to meet Bill. Tutt raised his gun high in the air,
and Bill shot from the hip. [*Bill never did shoot from the hip.*—
W.E.C.] The difference in the firing was caused by Tutt's
elevation of his gun, and the shots were so close together
that it sounded almost like one shot. After he was shot, Tutt
ran through the second arch of the court-house and out on
the sidewalk and fell. McClary and another man ran to him,
and when they reached him he was dead, shot through the
heart.

The circuit court for Greene County was in session at the
time. The account in the *History of Greene County* says that
as soon as Bill had fired, and saw that his shot had taken
effect, he handed over his pistols to the sheriff and surrendered himself. He was promptly indicted, arrested on a
bench warrant, and brought to trial. He was prosecuted by
the attorney for the commonwealth, Major R. W. Fyan, and

defended by Honorable John S. Phelps, at one time Governor
of Missouri. The empty chamber of Tutt's revolver was ex-
hibited to the jury, and, upon the ground of reasonable doubt
that Hickok was the aggressor, the jury acquitted him.
Tutt's friends were expecting trouble and were present to
avenge him. Tutt's brother knew that serious trouble was
impending and went to find Wild Bill and gave him a defiant
answer to a very reasonable request.

It was said at the time by some of the crowd that Hickok
was cleared because he was an ex-Federal soldier, and a radi-
cal in politics, and that the man he shot had been a rebel.
A lawyer, probably a rebel, harangued a crowd from the
balcony of the courthouse, advocating lynching, but nothing
came of it.

A study of all the evidence as preserved in the printed
records, it seems, should convince any candid, fair-minded
man; that Hickok was on the defensive for some time before
this killing, that he wished to avoid killing; that he gave due
notice that he would not permit his watch to be carried
across the Square; that he was defied by Tutt and his friends;
that Tutt fired, and may have fired first; that while Bill intended to kill Tutt if he persisted in carrying the watch
across the Square, he did not wish to kill, and gave Tutt's
younger brother a message designed to prevent trouble. And
when Wild Bill appeared on the Square, Tutt hurried to meet
him, still carrying the watch.

CHAPTER XV · *Wild Bill Returns to Kansas*

WILD BILL killed Dave Tutt July 21, 1865. The author of *Harper's Magazine* article came to Springfield a few days later and met Bill. His story was published in February 1867. When he went away, Bill was already famous, for the author wrote:

Whenever I had met an officer or soldier who had served in the Southwest I heard of Wild Bill and his exploits, until these stories became so frequent and of such an extraordinary character as to quite outstrip personal knowledge of adventure by camp and field; and the hero of these strange tales took shape in my mind as did Jack the Giant Killer or Sinbad the Sailor in childhood's days. As then, I now had the most implicit faith in the existence of the individual; but how one man could accomplish such prodigies of strength and feats of daring was a continued wonder.

He further testifies that his hero was called "Wild Bill, the Scout of the Plains" even at that time, and that the story of his life was "confirmed in all important points by many witnesses."

Wild Bill was in Springfield as late, at least, as January 25, 1866, for on that date one Orr, a policeman, killed James Coleman. Wild Bill saw the killing and was a witness at the hearing of Orr.

In the winter of 1865–66 there was trouble at Fort Riley. It was believed that officers there were short in their accounts. Horses and mules were being stolen from the Fort Riley stables, and desertion was increasing, many of the deserters riding away astride Government horses and mules. Captain Owens, put in command so establish order and

discipline, immediately sent to Springfield for Wild Bill. On
the recommendation of General Easton, Chief Quartermaster
at Fort Leavenworth, and of Captain Owens, Wild Bill was
appointed Deputy United States Marshal, in February 1866.
After a few weeks about Fort Riley, bringing order out of
chaos, Bill gave his attention to deserters and horse thieves.
His first trip was south through Council Grove to the upper
waters of the Little Arkansas. A few days later he returned.
He had no assistance, but he was driving nine mules and taking back two men, deserters. His brother, who was at Fort
Riley when he rode in, was amazed at what he believed was
Bill's carelessness, for the largest captive was riding a mule at
Bill's side.

"That man could reach over and draw one of your six-
shooters. Are you not afraid to take such chances?" asked
his brother.

"I am not afraid," replied Bill. "I could easily draw the
other revolver and shoot each of them dead before they
could fire a shot."

Dr. William Finlaw, Post Surgeon at Fort Riley, was
ordered to Fort McPherson in May 1866. A considerable
number of troops under General Sherman went from Fort
Leavenworth to Fort McPherson at the same time. Wild
Bill was the guide. While waiting at Marysville, he took the
little daughter of Dr. Finlaw with him to hunt bullfrogs along
the Blue River. They secured quite a number, and Bill gave
them to the Doctor, who turned them over to Lucy, their
cook. When she sprinkled salt on them they flounced about
the pan, which so frightened her that she dropped them. This
amused Bill.

It was at this time that Wild Bill saw once again the Rock
Creek Station where he had slain McCanles five years before.
Sherman camped one night on the river there. Frank Helvey
said:

I did not see Wild Bill again [after the killing of McCanles] until 1866 or 1867, when he was with General Sherman as a guide and escort. . . . They encamped for the night on the Little Sandy near our Station. Before they had got fairly settled, General Sherman with Wild Bill accompanying him, rode up to the Station and warned us not to let the soldiers have any whisky.

In the fall of 1866 Dr. Finlaw was recalled to Fort Riley. Wild Bill was again detailed as his escort, and was given only ten soldiers as a guard. So solicitous was he for the safety of Dr. Finlaw and family that he slept every night on blankets under their ambulance. When remonstrated with for his trouble he said: "Your children are in my care, and I would not have anything happen to them for the world. Think of Indians getting the baby!"

The next spring Dr. Finlaw's eldest daughter was at Fort Ellsworth. On her return to Fort Leavenworth the wagons stopped one night at the site of Abilene. She saw Stanley and Wild Bill there, and says in her letter to the writer: "It was during this night that Stanley took notes of Bill's part in the war. . . . I rode into the fort [Leavenworth] just three days after a command of troops, with Wild Bill as scout and Henry M. Stanley as correspondent, left on an Indian expedition." Her grandfather was George Snyder, who was a sutler at Forts Riley, Ellsworth, and Harker. In his diary she found this entry: "Henry M. Stanley and Wild Bill my guests until three A.M."

Kansas City was little more than a frontier post in 1866. She was conscious of rising commercial power and importance, but her customs, habits, social order, and general conditions were still those of pioneer days. Her saloons and gambling-houses were richly furnished, and business and professional men were often to be found there. Transactions involving immediate thousands and future millions were frequently made there. The crowds which surged through these places held cattlemen from Texas, mining-kings from

the Rockies, great freighters over the prairies and the mountains, the projectors of railroads over the Great Plains,
bankers, proprietors of infant stock-yards and packing in-
dustries destined to become the greatest in the world.

Wild Bill's business as Deputy United States Marshal
often took him to Leavenworth. On his first trip there from
Fort Riley he decided to go down to Kansas City. He went
by steamboat, and his coming was heralded. Jim Crow Chiles
was then king of the Kansas City sporting fraternity and
the underworld. As a "bad man" the town was of the opinion
he had no equal. People had to agree with Jim Crow or take
the consequences. He was a large man, but compact and
heavily muscled. He had killed men before, during, and after
the Civil War, always without much provocation, and without any trouble with the law. He had served under Quantrill,
Shelby, and Price, but would not submit to discipline and
was not a good soldier. It was supposed that Jim Crow and
Wild Bill would begin shooting on sight. Excitement prevailed. Crowds appeared on the bluffs to see Wild Bill's boat
come in. When it whistled in the turn of the Missouri at the
mouth of the Kaw, the crowds broke for the landing at the
foot of Delaware Street. From there the people followed Bill
as he sauntered into" Headquarters," the gambling establishment of which Jim Crow was manager. They saw Jim
Crow come forward, smiling. He said:

"How are you, Bill? I haven't seen you since your name
was Barnes and you gave us so much trouble as a spy. Glad
to see you now, though."

"Mighty glad to see you, Jim Crow. Haven't seen you
since we used to play poker in Price's army. Stake me to a
stack of chips—Jennison cleaned me out at Leavenworth."

"Certainly," said Jim Crow. "Here they are." And he
pushed them across the table. The crowd withdrew, feeling
cheated and righteously indignant.

But Jim Crow was a ruffian. Ordered by James Peacock, Marshal of Independence, to stop his noise on Sunday, he opened fire and was killed by Peacock.

At Leavenworth, Bill found many former comrades. He visited the extensive and well-appointed gambling-rooms fitted up by Colonel Jennison on Delaware Street. There he met Jack Harvey, "Sore-eyed" Dave, Jack Hays, Walt Sinclair, "One-eyed" Blunt, and other members of the Red Legs, many of whom had served with him. In fact, he had served with Red Legs so frequently that he was considered a member of their organization, though he never formally belonged to it.

Wild Bill also spent some of his time at the old Six-mile House, on the Leavenworth Road, in Wyandotte County, where he found his old-time friend and comrade, Theodore Bartles. It must not be forgotten that Bill had spent the first four years of his life in the West in Johnson County, Kansas, and within twenty miles of Kansas City. This, and the fact that so many of his old comrades and friends were in the vicinity, accounts for his choosing Kansas City as the center of his activities after the Civil War.

About this time, baseball was beginning to develop into a real American institution. A Kansas City Club was organized and named the "Antelopes." The principal men of the city were its members: D. F. Twitchell was president; William Warner, vice president; and W. H. Winants, secretary. The field was in the vicinity of Fourteenth Street about Oak and McGee Streets. On the Saturday afternoons when games were played, there was a holiday by common consent. There was no enclosure and no fee for admission. Everybody was welcome. Chied Speers sometimes had trouble to keep the crowds off the "diamond" when the game became close and interesting, but they were good-natured.

The Antelopes were invincible; everything went down

before them—for a time. At Atchison, one Sunday afternoon,
they were beaten, wallowed in the dust by the "Pomeroys."
They took their defeat with true sporting spirit and invited
the Pomeroys to Kansas City for another game. This time
the Pomeroys were defeated, and a near-riot resulted. The
umpire saved himself by flight, and the game ended with
much bad feeling. The headline in the *Times* was "The Town
Disgraced." The Pomeroys apologized and the Antelopes
invited them back for another game, the following Saturday.

Wild Bill was an enthusiast for games of sport, and especially for baseball. He was an authority on the technique
of the game as played in that day, so was invited to be the
umpire of the game. He consented, and when the Antelopes
were ready, he was sent for. He was found at Jake Forcade's
gambling rooms, at Fourth and Main Streets, playing poker
with one of the founders of the city. He hurried out to the
grounds and directed the game. Not a protest was made
from any of his decisions. There was no dissatisfaction from
any quarter. The Pomeroys were defeated by a score of 48
to 28. At the end of the game Wild Bill was asked to name the
price of his services. "Send down to Frank Short's livery for
an open hack and two white horses to carry me back to
Jake's." The hack soon appeared with Short's crack team of
white horses, and his compliments for "the distinguished
guest of Kansas City for the day." Wild Bill returned to the
city in state.

The Kansas Pacific Railroad, now the Union Pacific, was
under construction from the mouth of the Kansas River
westward up that stream in 1866. It reached Fort Riley in
October, and in November it passed Junction City. The construction of the track had gone forward rapidly and Fort
Harker was officially proclaimed on the eleventh of November, though the railroad was not operated to that point until
June 6, 1867.

Wild Bill began to travel up and down the Kansas Pacific in 1866. He was at Fort Harker when it was officially named. He made the acquaintance of the principal contractors for the railroad in Kansas City and Wyandotte, and friendships then formed endured in many instances to death.

CHAPTER XVI · *Wild Bill in Hancock's Indian War*

FORT RILEY lost many horses. The soldiers could not find the thieves nor recover the stolen stock. Often they did not themselves return, but deserted and rode into the wilderness on Government horses. In January 1867, Wild Bill, with a small force of scouts selected by himself from the forces at the Fort, invaded the Solomon Valley and came back down the Republican. He brought no prisoners, but he recovered more than two hundred horses and mules. His report stated that some of the worst of the horse thieves had had recourse to firearms but that they would not trouble the Border further.

Upon his return from Solomon, in January 1867, Wild Bill was sent into the country north of the railroad west of Fort Riley to put a stop to the theft of timber from Government lands. This timber was being cut for railroad cross-ties, which were sold to the contractors building the Kansas Pacific. By the first of April he had taken into custody John Hobbs and twenty-eight others, his last arrests having been made on Paradise Creek. The prisoners were lodged in the Topeka jail and were tried the following summer, but as Bill and the other deputies were on the Plains as scouts for the army, evidence against them could not then be secured, and they were acquitted.

Mr. Nicolay had knowledge of another incident in the life of Wild Bill in the winter of 1867–68. He was detailed to guard a stagecoach from the vicinity of Fort Larned to Burlingame, Kansas, on the Old Santa Fé Trail. It was

96

[THE LAST SHOT, FROM A CURRIER AND IVES PRINT]

shortly after the great snow which prevented the Nineteenth Kansas from reaching General Sheridan at Camp Supply, and the weather was extremely cold. West of Council Grove Bill noticed that the horses seemed out of control of the driver, a young man from Missouri. Bill stopped the horses and spoke to the driver, who said that his hands and feet were frozen. Bill put the driver inside the coach, tied his own horse to the back of the stage, mounted the driver's seat, and drove on. At Council Grove no physician could be found to attend the frozen limbs of the driver, so Bill drove the coach to Burlingame and pulled up at the Bratton Hotel. Bill himself was almost frozen, but his thoughts were not for himself. He called for help to get the young driver in the Hotel and started off to find a doctor. Doctor Hart was finally located and he examined the frozen limbs. He said the boy would die if his left leg was not amputated immediately, as it was frozen solid. He had very little chloroform, and it would be necessary for some one or more to hold the boy while his leg was taken off. Bill held him and a Mrs. Kenney, who was in charge of the hotel, was the Doctor's helper. The three of them amputated the frozen limb.

General Sherman was in command of the Department embracing the Great Plains. Early in the year 1867, he designated General Hancock to take charge of the Indian War. General Hancock was a fine office-soldier, a wonderful drawing-room soldier. But the situation now confronting him was Indian warfare, and he was not fitted to meet it.

At Fort Leavenworth General Hancock did two sensible things. One was to select General Custer as commander of his fighting forces, and the other was to employ a number of plainsmen and some Delaware Indians as scouts and trail-followers. He arrived at Fort Riley by rail, bringing artillery and six companies of infantry. There Custer joined him with four companies of the Seventh Cavalry and one company of

the Thirty-seventh Infantry. Hancock marched from Fort
Riley to Fort Harker, ninety miles up the Smoky Hill. Then
with two troops of cavalry added to his army he marched to
Fort Larned, some seventy miles to the southwest.

Hancock went to Fort Larned for the reason that the
Cheyennes and the Sioux were camped on the Pawnee Fork
about thirty miles above Fort Larned. But the Indians,
having the Chivington massacre fresh in mind, and being
cautious, promptly fled at his approach. Hancock moved on
from Fort Larned, and on April 14, met a large body of
Indians near Pawnee Fork. The Cheyenne Chiefs who had
advanced from the Indian line were Roman Nose, who bore a
white flag, Bull Bear, White Horse, Gray Beard, and Medicine Wolf. Representing the Sioux were Pawnee Killer and
six others. Hancock inquired if the Indians wished to fight.
The Chiefs said they were friendly. Hancock camped near
the Indian villages. He sent Guerrier, his half-breed scout
and interpreter, to remain in the village during the night and
to report every two hours. At nine-thirty Guerrier reported
that when he left the village the Indians were saddling up to
leave and that they were destroying their lodges.

Hancock ordered General Custer to take the trail in pursuit early the following morning. General Custer started at
five o'clock, on the fifteenth, with four squadrons of the
Seventh Cavalry and followed the trail rapidly in the direction of Walnut Creek. The Indians fearing that Custer would
overtake them, broke into small bands and fled in every
direction. On the sixteenth, Custer continuing his march
in pursuit of the Indians, struck the Smoky Hill thirteen
miles west of Downer's Station. There he learned that the
Indians had been crossing the Smoky Hill in bands since the
morning of the sixteenth of April. They had attacked and
captured Lookout Station, the first mail station west of Fort
Hays, killing the three men at that station and partly burn-

ing their bodies. They had burned the station-house. Custer notified Hancock that these outrages had been committed by the Indians who had abandoned their villages on Pawnee Fork. Having insufficient forage and supplies, Custer was compelled to return to Fort Hays.

On the nineteenth, General Hancock burned the Indian villages on the Pawnee Fork in revenge for the depredations on the Smoky Hill, and started his return march to Fort Leavenworth, which he reached on the ninth of May. From there he issued orders for an expedition of cavalry under Custer from Fort Hays north at the earliest possible date.

Thus ended Hancock's operations against the Plains Tribes in 1867. A General with a knowledge of Indian character might have prevented a war, but the blustering march of General Hancock on the Sioux and Cheyenne villages on the North Fork of Pawnee Creek was taken by them to mean that he intended to repeat the Sand Creek massacre. The Indians out-maneuvered Hancock, made him ridiculous, and then marched away north to continue war. No blame can attach to any of the officers or soldiers under Hancock. They did their duty and obeyed orders.[1]

In the Hancock campaign Wild Bill bore an important part. He was attached to the command as scout at Fort Riley where Hancock found him acting as Deputy U. S. Marshal. He was constantly riding the country in front of the command. He entered the Indian camps and followed Indian warriors from point to point. He made many trips to Fort Hays, and returned. How he escaped the Indians is something he could not himself explain. Later he told Captain Henry C. Lindsay of the Eighteenth Kansas that in this scouting for General Hancock he passed through more danger every twenty-four hours than he had ever encountered in any week's service in the Civil War. He did not dare ride by day, but had to make all his trips at night, hiding in some

gully, ravine, or clump of bushes during the day. Bands of
Indians often passed within pistol shot. Both he and his
horse suffered intensely from cold and thirst, from fatigue
and the lack of food.

While scouting once close in the rear of the retreating
Indians ahead of Custer, six warriors by mere chance rode
into the clump of trees at the head of a ravine where Bill was
hiding.[2] It was necessary for him to act at once, for the Indians would have ridden over him in three minutes. He
stepped over his horse and shot the foremost Indian, which
was the first notice the savages had of his presence. They
fled, but Bill killed two of them before they were beyond
range. The others escaped. He knew that it would be only a
few minutes until more Indians would appear, and he rode
swiftly down the shallow ravine.

Having gone a mile he dismounted and cautiously crawled
to the top of the bank. Looking over the prairie, he could see
a straggling band of warriors, and women with the travois
and children, all hurrying north toward the Smoky Hill.
Seeing that he was in the line of march, he decided to get to
safer ground. A small ravine came in from the south and up
this he led his horse. When Bill could no longer proceed along
the ravine without being seen he mounted and rode out on
the prairie, and at that instant a band of Indians appeared
almost in front of him. He could not return to the ravine for
the Indians had seen him. At this instant a band of Indians
appeared at some distance east of the first band. Bill decided
to run directly south and pass between the bands. This he
did, but the Indians were pressing him closely as he cleared
the gap. They followed. Bill soon saw that his horse would
distance them and pulled him in. He permitted the Indians
to approach within range, when he killed three of them, but
as the others gave no indication of abandoning the chase,
he put spurs to his horse and was soon out of range.

CHAPTER XVII · *Custer and Wild Bill*

THE plan of campaign of General Custer was to scout the country from Fort Hays north to Fort McPherson on the Platte; thence describe a semicircle to the southwest, touching the headwaters of the Republican; reaching the Platte near Fort Sedgwick; and from Fort Wallace, back to Fort Hays—a distance of more than a thousand miles. General Custer left Fort Hays on the first day of June with about 350 men and a train of twenty wagons, going in the direction of Fort McPherson, distant 225 miles. This campaign is brilliantly described in Custer's *Wild Life on the Plains.* Just enough of its features are given here to furnish the necessary background and so render intelligible Wild Bill's part in it.

Custer had it in mind to offer some inducement to bring the Sioux into camp near Fort McPherson. To this plan the Sioux consented, but they did not keep their promise. General Sherman, arriving on the day following the council, ordered Custer to move toward the Forks of the Republican. General Custer was to scout the country thoroughly, after which he was to march to Fort Sedgwick. General Sherman supposed he might be at the latter post when Custer arrived.

The country was swarming with hostile Indians and terrific outrages and atrocities were of daily occurrence. Custer himself was constantly attacked. Wagon-trains carrying supplies were nearly impossible to get through the Indian country. Only the most daring and clever dispatch-bearers had a chance. The Indians were willing to parley. But they demanded arms and ammunition and refused any peaceful

101

terms. The story of Custer's campaign is a long one. But, unlike Hancock, he understood Indian warfare perfectly.

The first day of July, Custer and his troops were about fifty miles west of Fort Sedgwick. Seeking to ascertain whether Sherman had left later orders than those sent by Major Elliott, Custer telegraphed Fort Sedgwick. He was informed that the day after Elliott had departed, Lieutenant Kidder, with ten men of the Second U. S. Cavalry, and Red Bead, a loyal Sioux, for guide, had been sent out with important dispatches for him. Custer had moved from the Forks of the Republican before the arrival of Kidder, and he requested that the later orders be telegraphed him.

Custer felt great anxiety for Lieutenant Kidder and his party and started immediately to his rescue. In the valley of the South Beaver, buzzards were seen flying in circles to the southwest. And at the point where the trail crossed the South Beaver the bodies of Lieutenant Kidder and his ten men were found, horribly mutilated and shot full of arrows. The body of Red Bead was there, his scalp lying beside him. The party had been attacked by the Sioux under Pawnee Killer and all slain. A trench was dug and the dead soldiers were buried where they fell.

General Custer reached Fort Wallace the day after finding the bodies of Lieutenant Kidder and his party. He found that the Indians had attacked the fort twice in the past few days and that in both engagements soldiers and Indians had been killed. The activities of the Indians about Fort Wallace had stopped all travel over the Smoky Hill route. No dispatches awaited General Custer at Fort Wallace. The terminus of the railroad was two hundred miles to the east, and the food at the fort was unfit for use. Cholera was epidemic and men were dying.

Custer decided to go to Fort Harker and obtain supplies. He left with a wagon-train and escort on the evening of the

fifteenth of July. Many of the stations between Fort Wallace
and Fort Hays were found in ruins, having been burned by
the Indians. Custer was compelled to march at night to
avoid attack. He knew they were watching every movement
of the train and its escort, which was attacked six miles
west of Downer's Station and two men killed. Fort Hays was
reached on the morning of the eighteenth. At Hays Custer
left Captain Hamilton with the train to rest one day with
orders to follow on to Fort Harker with Colonels Cook and
Tom Custer. With two troops of cavalry General Custer
pressed on to Fort Harker, reaching that post in a ride of
less than twelve hours. At Fort Harker he telegraphed Fort
Sedgwick announcing the death of Kidder and his party. He
found General A. J. Smith in command at Fort Harker and
made a report of all his movements. It was arranged that
Captain Hamilton should be furnished the supplies and that
his train should start back at once for Fort Wallace. General
Custer applied for permission to visit Fort Riley where he
expected to meet Mrs. Custer, and this was granted.

This ended the activities of General Custer for the time
being. The complete failure of the Hancock campaign made
it necessary that some victim be found. The blame was to be
shifted. General Custer was arrested for going on from Fort
Harker to Fort Riley. Here was something for General Hancock to do. In any warfare against a fellow-soldier or West-
Pointer General Hancock was superb. General Custer, who
had been left to his own resources and had made dangerous
marches, the only officer who had shown intelligence, was
now seized, charged with grave offenses, and court-martialed.
His sentence was suspension from the army for one year.

General A. J. Smith had been left at Fort Hays by Hancock. It was necessary for him to be constantly advised of
Custer's movements, and to this end Wild Bill was made the
courier to ride between Fort Hays and Custer. It was a task

at which the bravest might well have hesitated. Jack Harvey was Bill's "pal." They were sometimes together, but were often compelled to ride the Plains separately and alone.

Bill was troubled much by Indians and delayed on one trip. He had been out three days. Lying concealed in a coulee, one noon he heard a low rumbling noise. He knew a herd of buffaloes was stampeding, and a cautious look revealed them coming directly toward him. To remain meant that he would be trampled to death, and he mounted and rode out on the prairie. As the herd was passing Indians appeared in pursuit. There was no way to escape their sight. Bill galloped east away from the thundering herd. Three Indians were bearing down on him. He knew there were others and that he must fight. Pulling in his horse, he permitted the Indians to gain on him slowly. At their first shots he halted and turned. The Indians slowed down. Bill shot the foremost and the others ran in different directions. Two more Indians now appeared. They were pushing their ponies and were soon in range and firing. Bill's trained pony dropped to the ground and he lay down behind him. The Indians were joined by the two first seen—four now. They began to circle around Bill and to shoot at him, but would not come into range. After a time Bill rolled over as though struck and lay still. When the Indians approached, Bill shot three of them.

Bill knew other Indians would be on his trail. He rode south and across the Republican. Coming out on the south bank, he saw a band of seven Indians approaching rapidly from the north. Bill urged his pony to its swiftest. The race was for miles, and Bill's horse began to tire and fail. One Indian was outriding his companions. He was mounted on a splendid pony—larger than usual, swift and untiring. The Indian gained despite all Bill could do. Suddenly Bill's pony stumbled and fell. The Indian was upon him before he could disengage himself and it was a hand-to-hand encounter. After

[DISTRIBUTION OF RATIONS TO THE INDIANS, FROM AN OLD PRINT]

a terrific struggle, Bill managed to stab the Indian to death. He threw himself on the Indian's pony and bore down on the remaining Indians who had been too fearful for a very close approach. He killed one of the Indians, but the others ran across the Republican. Bill was only too glad to see them go and did not pursue. The next morning he rode into Custer's camp, without further molestation.

In the afternoon of a hot day Wild Bill and Jack Harvey were nearing Fort Hays. Some thirty miles out they found a man wounded and scalped. He died in a few minutes. He said a band of fifteen Indians had attacked a party of six men, of whom he was one. He was shot and fell from his horse, but he knew nothing of what had happened to his companions. They left this man and rode on. In a few minutes a cloud of dust rose to the north and soon the Indian band emerged, coming down before them like a whirlwind. They looked about for cover and found a depression which became a ravine lower down. The scouts hurried their horses into this little ravine and waited. The Indians seemed to expect them to keep on down the ravine and rode close by. Bill killed two and Harvey three before the Indians could wheel and dodge back. Nothing happened for some time and so Bill looked out over the top. The Indians were far out on the prairie. The scouts thought they might escape now without further trouble and went down the ravine to its junction with a larger one. This they descended until it came out into the flat dry bed of a stream. Riding across this stretch of sand to a slight elevation they saw the Indians bearing down upon them at great speed.

They lost no time before flight but the screeching Indians seemed to be out-running them. Harvey looked back, got their position and fired his revolver over his shoulder. An Indian dropped from his pony. Bill then selected an Indian and fired over his shoulder as they ran, and his Indian fell.

The Indians pulled up their ponies. Bill proposed that they turn and charge the Indians, which they did. The Indians turned and fled, and the scouts thought best to let them go.

Theodore Bartles had a quarrel with a citizen of Old Wyandotte. The man became a post-trader at a Western fort. Bartles went up the Kansas Pacific to seek his adversary and kill him on sight. By chance he met Wild Bill at Hays. Bill and Bartles were more than friends. They had scouted together and fought together in the Civil War, for Bartles was one of the famous band of Red Legs. Wild Bill was glad to see his old friend. When he learned from Bartles the object of his appearance on the Plains, he prevailed on him to relinquish it. But being afraid to leave him to his own reflections at Hays, Bill induced Bartles and Walt Sinclair, who had come out with him to see justice done, to accompany him and Jack Harvey on the scout to Custer's Camp at the Forks of the Republican.

The party arrived at Custer's Camp after Custer had departed for Fort Sedgwick. Wild Bill was as keen in following the trail as an Indian. Bartles, tired of riding by night and sleeping by day, insisted on riding by day, having never scouted on the Plains and not knowing the hazard of it. Bill consented to it with the greatest reluctance, for he knew that the country was swarming with Sioux and Cheyennes. Late in the afternoon of the second day a small band of Indians crossed their trail. They ran over the Plain some miles and disappeared over a low ridge. When the scouts came to the crest of this ridge they saw below them perhaps a hundred warriors, apparently in ambush. The scouts hurriedly turned and ran north with the whole band of Indians in eager, deadly pursuit. They were at a disadvantage, for their horses, after a long day, were pretty well tired out. It required but a few minutes to convince them that they would be overtaken, so they concluded to turn and fight. The scouts rode straight for the center of the Indian line, but did not fire until they were within twenty feet of the foe. As each one was a dead shot, every bullet brought down a warrior.

The Indians separated into two bands. The scouts rode between them, not knowing how many they killed. They did not stop after having broken through the Indian line, so the Indians turned and again pursued. But now they rode with more caution, taking care not to come within pistol-shot, though they could easily have ridden the scouts down. The scouts stopped on an elevation in which there was a slight depression, and the Indians began to circle around them. The scouts were firing from behind their prostrate horses. Bill watched the Indians ride a few minutes. As an Indian rode his pony by he put his head up to get a view and Bill killed him. The pony ran on in the circle.

Bill did a daring thing. He mounted his jaded horse and rode toward the line of circling warriors. As he swooped to pick up the pony's drag-rope a Sioux warrior fired at him, and reached to take the pony's rope. Two other Indians now righted themselves to erect positions on their ponies. They charged Bill, who was running with the circle and he killed them both. Having the pony under control, Bill began to pull away from the Indian circle in the direction of his comrades. This feat changed the battle. The Indians broke their circle and came on in a mass. In the mêlée Bill seized the drag-ropes of two more ponies, which he brought in.

These Indian horses were comparatively fresh, and the scouts transferred their trappings to them. They mounted and charged down the hill, meeting the Indians at the plain. They fired as they came on, and opened a way through the Indian mass. Having cleared the Indians, the scouts ran for life. The Indians' pursuit was relentless and for miles it was uncertain whether or not the scouts would escape. Far on the sky-line in their way appeared another line, perhaps Indians, and the situation became desperate. But the only hope was in riding straight ahead, for the Indians had also seen the wavering intangible line. The line grew and became a solid reality. It rose into a sea of buffalo, in a mad stampede. The scouts could not evade it. They had to meet it. They opened fire as they plunged in, and as dead buffalo piled up the herd split and passed about them. When the rolling mass had gone and the stifling dust-cloud had drifted away, not an Indian was in sight. The scouts did not stop for the night but kept to the trail. In the gray light of the morning they saw far to the north the low lines of Fort Sedgwick.

CHAPTER XVIII · *Wild Bill in 1868*

A T THE beginning of the year 1868 Wild Bill was in the service of the Government with headquarters at Fort Hays. Frank A. Root, a pioneer in Kansas and joint author with this writer of *The Overland Stage to California*, said in the *Atchison Daily Free Press*, January 6, 1868:

In Hays I formed the acquaintance of William Hickok, better known as "Wild Bill." He is a man of about thirty years of age, over six feet high, straight as an arrow, with long black hair hanging over his shoulders. He is in the employ of the Government as a detective, and is probably better acquainted with the Plains than any man living.

April 11, 1868, the *Junction City Union* copied the following item from the *Topeka Leader:*

W. F. Cody, government detective, and Wm. Haycock (Hickok), Deputy U. S. Marshal, brought eleven prisoners and lodged them in our calaboose on Monday last—a band of robbers having their headquarters on the Solomon, charged with stealing Government property and desertion.

The Indian War of 1868 was a continuation of that of 1867. The Medicine Lodge treaty, with the Kiowas, Comanches, Cheyennes, Arapahoes, and Apaches, made in October 1867, had a special bearing on events the following year.

The Medicine Lodge was near the present town of that name in Barber County, Kansas. There were about five thousand Indians present at the sessions of the Peace Commission: Comanches, 150 lodges; Kiowas, 150 lodges; Arapahoes, 175 lodges; Kiowas and Apaches, 85 lodges; and Cheyennes, 250 lodges. For a month prior to the meeting the Indian Department had been gathering near the Lodge a great amount of material to be given to the Indians as presents. A large herd of cattle was driven to the treaty-grounds and held for the Indians. Food—coffee, sugar, flour, and dried fruits in quantity sufficient for an army campaign—was stored there to feed the Indians.

What Indians? The Indians that had been murdering settlers, scalping women and children, killing workers on the railroads, burning houses and stage stations, attacking forts and laying waste the frontier all the summer of 1867. These Indians had attacked Custer, Hamilton and the wagon trains, had murdered Lieutenant Kidder and his escort, and had fought pitched battles at the gates of Fort Wallace. Now they presented themselves to the Peace Commission and proclaimed themselves friendly Indians with love in their hearts for the white people. Knowing all the outrages these Indians had committed on the border settlements, the Commission still received them as good Indians and made treaties with them. Even the Indians were astounded at the prodigality of the Great Father. They could not carry away all that was given them. Much was left on the prairies to rot.

Then, the greatest gift of all was brought out. It was the ammunition. They had used up their entire supply along the frontier, killing settlers and ranchmen and railroad workmen, and it was magnanimous of the Great Father to load them up for another campaign. The Indians were hardly to be blamed for believing the Government liked to have them drench the border in blood.

The ammunition issued to the Indians at Medicine Lodge was used up and shot away during the winter of 1867–68. When spring arrived the Indians were practically without ammunition. The Peace Commission had promised that more should be given them in the spring. So in the spring, the Indians left their winter quarters along the streams in the western part of what is now Oklahoma, and gathered about the agencies and forts along the Arkansas River.

After settling in their camps about the forts, the Indians became insistent that the arms and ammunition promised them at Medicine Lodge should be delivered. Meantime they were eating good meals three times a day from food furnished them by the Government. This war material was finally distributed from Fort Larned. Within three days after receiving it the Indians started north on their work of death. They struck the settlements along the Smoky Hill and the Saline, laying waste stations, ranches, and farms. Continuing on their way they soon appeared in the Valleys of the Solomon and the Republican.

The situation was desperate. The country from the Arkansas north to the Republican was filled with Indian bands committing hideous crimes without restraint.

Early in September, Colonel George A. Forsyth, of General Sheridan's staff, Lieutenant Beecher, and Dr. Moore, with forty-seven scouts, left Fort Wallace in pursuit of the Cheyennes under Chief Roman Nose and the Sioux under Pawnee Killer. On September 17, this body of troops was attacked on the Arickaree Fork of the North Republican. There was fought there in the next few days the battle of the Arickaree, one of the outstanding battles of Indian warfare. Chief Roman Nose was killed. Forsyth was dangerously wounded. Daring scouts succeeded in breaking through the Indian line and reaching Fort Wallace. Reinforcements were dispatched and Forsyth and his surviving scouts rescued.

For the people of Kansas the condition became unbearable. Governor Crawford applied to the United States Government for authority to raise one regiment of troops to defend the Kansas frontier. Authority to do this was granted, and he organized the Nineteenth Kansas Regiment.

General Sheridan had been appointed to the command of the district embracing Kansas, Nebraska and Oklahoma. General Hancock had been permitted to return to Washington. It was the plan of General Sheridan to make a winter campaign against the Indians while they were lying inactive in their villages. The Cheyennes, Arapahoes, Comanches, Kiowas, and Prairie Apaches had been driven from the bloody Kansas frontier by the cold weather and were encamped for the winter along the Washita in what is now Oklahoma.

One of Sheridan's first acts was to call General Custer back into service September 24, 1868. He was then at his home in Northern Ohio. The following day he took train for the West. He stopped at Leavenworth one day and arrived at Fort Hays on the morning of September 30, 1868. General Sheridan had transferred his headquarters from Fort Leavenworth to Fort Hays, from which point the campaign was conducted until the first of November. General Custer went on to assume command of the Seventh Cavalry, which was then in camp on Bluff Creek thirty miles south of Fort Dodge. So bold were the Indians that they were attacking the regiment every day. Fort Dodge was to be the base of supplies for the campaign General Sheridan was planning for the winter of 1868–69. It was decided to establish a temporary base about one hundred miles south of Fort Dodge. It was named Camp Supply.

Custer's arrival at Camp Supply was the eighteenth of November, and on the twenty-first, General Sheridan arrived. It was necessary to act promptly, giving no time for the Indians on the Washita to become informed of Sheridan's plans. On the evening of November 22, orders were issued for the Seventh Cavalry to move promptly at daylight on the morning of the twenty-third. In the meantime, Governor Crawford was marching to join them, hampered by snow and terrible cold, and lack of adequate supplies. He arrived at Camp Supply on the twenty-sixth.

General Custer left Camp Supply on the twenty-third, in

search of the Indian towns. The villages were reached on the morning of the twenty-seventh, on the head waters of the Washita. Custer divided his troops into four detachments, all to approach the Indian town from different directions. The attack was entirely successful. The Indians were defeated and their villages destroyed. It was a Cheyenne town and many were killed, including Black Kettle, the most famous of the Cheyenne Chiefs. Large numbers of horses were captured. Captive women and children were assembled and cared for. The Indians camped below on the Washita, immediately moved south and were pursued by General Custer, who came up with them at Fort Cobb. Eight hundred ponies captured at Black Kettle's village were slain. The captives were sent north by General Sheridan to Fort Hays, where they were confined in a stockade. The foregoing is the brief review of the conditions on the frontier in the summer and fall of 1868, necessary to a knowledge of the services of Wild Bill during that time.

Wild Bill was in all the operations of the army against the Indians in 1868.[1] He was not made chief scout for Custer for the reason that he could not be spared from the dangerous work of keeping open the lines of communication between the army and the posts, so he missed the battle of the Washita, greatly to his regret. He was the courier upon whom alone the army officers depended for getting their dispatches through from point to point, from post to post, from command to command. No other man could be prevailed on to attempt this dangerous duty. Death rode beside any scout of that day from the moment the gate of one fort closed behind him until he rode into the gate of another.

During this scouting, night became more familiar to Wild Bill than the daylight. Bill could speak the language of every Plains tribe. In the villages of some of the tribes he had friends as well as deadly enemies. He crept stealthily into

many a village, in search of information for the Government,
where his life depended on the flutter of a wing, the movement of a sleeping dog, or the tossing head of a drowsy
pony. He went into the lodges of those whom he had be-
friended, conversed a few minutes, and left, knowing that a
misstep or the breaking of a twig under his feet meant death.
He was the scout on whom the army depended for intelligence of what was transpiring in the country through which
it passed. He kept communications unbroken between Camp
Supply, Fort Dodge, Fort Larned, and Fort Hays.

General Custer did not return from the pursuit of the
Cheyennes until the spring of 1869. At that time William D.
Street, a pioneer in Northwestern Kansas, was making a
tour of the Plains. The entry in his journal relative to that
event reads as follows:

One noteworthy incident of the trip was the meeting of "Wild Bill" (J. B
Hickok), the famous scout. He was the bearer of dispatches to General
Custer, and also for Fort Dodge, who met us south of Fort Hays. . . . He
was to my mind the greatest and bravest frontiersman of his time.

General Sheridan had in mind an expedition into the
Indian country north from Fort Wallace. It was the country
then ranged over by the Sioux, and the warriors of that
tribe were hostile. Wild Bill was ordered to scout through
the Sioux country to ascertain and report on conditions
there. He left Fort Hays alone about the first of August 1868,
taking the Hays-McPherson trail. No Indians were encountered north of Fort Hays, and at the crossing of the
Republican he turned west and penetrated the Sioux do-
main.

In the vicinity of Custer's old camp at the Forks of the
Republican he found many trails recently made and other
evidences that the country was swarming with Indians uneasy and hostile. The old road to Fort Sedgwick showed constant use, with interlacing trails crossing it at all angles. A

large band had passed west over it not more than twenty-four hours before Bill's arrival. This main trail he followed.

Near midnight he came up to a culmination of ridges or low-lying divides. The night was dark, but Bill made out, as he believed, the lines of an Indian camp lying far over against the bank or bluff of a stream. He rode in that direction with extra care. Stealthily he approached, for no Indian camp is ever in complete repose. Once in the camp, his caution increased, for ponies were tied at lodge doors, dogs were sleeping in the grass, and sometimes an inmate of a lodge would stir. Not all the Indians were under cover, some of them lying rolled in blankets and sleeping outside. In the center of the camp a light appeared. A lodge-flap was raised and men entered. It required some minutes for Bill to reach this lodge, but he knew that the chiefs and some of the principal warriors were inside in council, and soon he heard enough to know that the Sioux were in daily communication with the Indians on the Arkansas, and that they knew conditions at the forts along the frontier.

As Bill passed a lodge near the edge of the camp a warrior came out. He stopped and faced Bill, discovering then that he was a white man. The Indian produced a knife and struck savagely at Bill, who threw his knife to guard. Bill being first to recover, struck the Indian, driving his knife deep into his breast. The commotion roused the camp. Indians cried out—"Pawnees! Pawnees! Watch the ponies!" Squaws uttered shrill cries. Warriors sounded their quavering war-cry. They rode like the wind in an ever widening circle about the village. Bill was soon enclosed and was uncertain as to whether he could escape.

A yelling Indian mounted on a powerful pony passed and Bill leaped up behind him. Before the warrior knew what had happened, Bill's knife was in his heart. Bill pushed him from the pony and rode with the circle twice about the

village before he found an opportunity to break away. He
fled toward Fort Sedgwick on the Indian pony. As the day
broke he secreted himself and horse in a canyon. During the
day he saw Indians riding in different directions, but none
came his way. At night he turned back toward Fort Wallace,
which point he finally reached in safety. In detailing this adventure to Colonel Lindsay, Bill always counted it among the
most dangerous and thrilling he ever had.

Wild Bill was known in all the tribes of the Plains. Some
of them gave him tribal names which they deemed expressive
of his actions against them. They feared him. He had been
in their grasp many times, but had slipped away and disappeared in a manner so unexpected that they came to believe him the favored one of some powerful Manitou.

Wild Bill was at Fort Lyon, Colorado, the winter of
1868–69, having been sent there with the Fifth Infantry
immediately after returning from his lone scout beyond the
Republican. But he was still the main dependence for getting dispatches through the Indian country. On one occasion
this winter, he was sent from Fort Lyon with dispatches to
General Sheridan, whom he found at Fort Cobb. Sheridan
had important information which it was necessary to send
to Fort Hays, and he gave the dispatches to Wild Bill to
carry to that point before returning to Fort Lyon.

In some way the Indians at Fort Cobb knew when he set
out on this long and perilous journey. A band of famous
killers was selected to follow him. They trailed like phan-
toms—unseen, but hovering near. Bill felt their presence,
although he could detect nothing. He rode slowly at times to
see if anything might appear. Then he would race his horse,
thinking to draw the trailers out if any there should be.

This continued until he crossed the Cimarron. In that
country he lay by one night and took the trail the next
morning to see what might develop. About the middle of the

forenoon he saw a dust-cloud on the trail in front of him—
to the north. He rode aside and stood behind the cut bank of
a prairie wash. Emerging from the rising dust there came
five Indians. They were searching the trail as they came, and
Bill concluded that they had passed him in the night, had
found it out by the absence of his trail, and that they were
now returning in search for him.

As the Indians approached, Bill rose and opened fire with
his repeating rifle. The Indians were taken by surprise and
Bill killed three before they were out of range. They had
wheeled, and they ran north. Bill was just mounting his
horse when he saw another dust-cloud. It was far to the
north of the fleeing warriors. Soon five warriors were to be
seen sweeping down the trail like a whirlwind.

Wild Bill never deceived himself. He knew when to run.
He rode behind a slight elevation to the west. This concealed
him and he was able to pass the Indians and get the trail
north of them. They halted where their comrades lay dead
and began to circle about to discover their terrible enemy.
It was some time before they found Bill's trail and compre-
hended his strategy, but when they followed his track into
the trail they knew he had again escaped and was far ahead
of them.

It was some time before the Indians came into sight again.
Looking back from a rise Bill saw them coming like the
wind. He was going at a fair gait, which he did not increase, for the Arkansas was yet far away, and he did not
wish to tire his horse. Two Indians now began to ride at an
angle to the trail. Soon two did the same on the other side of
the trail. It was their object to pass him on the sides and wait
on the trail in front. He slowed down. When the side runners
came even with him he charged the two on his right. They
turned, but he killed one. The other turned back to those on
the main trail. The two at his left were pressing forward now

and kept him out of the trail. He was compelled to run over the Plain. This placed him at a disadvantage and the Indians gained. He charged the two on his left, and, before they could wheel their ponies, he killed one of them. He pursued the others and this brought him back to the trail, but the Indian escaped.

Four warriors were now coming up the trail, but they were careful to keep out of range. The fifth Indian soon joined them. Bill hoped to hold them off until he reached the Arkansas, but that was now an hour away. It seemed much longer, but finally he saw the white sand swirling in the wind and knew that beyond lay the river. The warriors began to fear their quarry would escape. Their ponies were weary but by unmerciful whipping they forced them to new speed. All parties came into the sand-hills about the same time. Bill dismounted at the ford and led his horse behind a pair of dunes. He saw the Indians slipping from one hill to the other. When they came in range, he began to fire. He killed two Indians, and the third did not show himself. And one was above the ford. This one soon came to view far out in the river making for the north side. It was a long shot, but true, and the warrior fell from his pony.

There was one more. Indian. Bill put his hat on the end of his gun barrel, and pushed it above the dune. Several minutes passed and it was not shot at. Bill then looked over the top. Far to the south he saw the lone Indian forcing his pony to some speed down the trail. Bill did not follow. He crossed the river and was soon at Fort Dodge.

CHAPTER XIX · *Wild Bill in 1869—to July*

I N 1868 one Gomer had built a sawmill on Kiowa Creek about fifty miles southeast of Denver, where thirty families lived. On a Sunday afternoon in September 1868, a courier rode by the Gomer residence saying that the Cheyennes and Arapahoes were on the warpath. An hour before he reached the Gomer mill he had seen on the Plains a prairie schooner, partly burned, and about it, the charred bodies of immigrants. A few days later some boys, playing on the sand-bar below the mill, saw a man appear on horseback, shouting "Indians!" The boys ran toward the mill, but the smallest one was unable to keep up and was captured. The following day about twenty men went out to find the boy. On the third day two Mexicans found his body. He had been shot and thrown into a bunch of sage brush.

Wild Bill, then at Fort Lyon[1] with the Fifth Cavalry, was sent out to scout north through what is now Eastern Colorado and return *via* Fort Wallace. On his way he passed through the Gomer settlement where the men were organizing to defend themselves from the increasing hostility of the Indians. Wild Bill was earnestly requested to take command of this company of volunteers for a few days, which he did, and they scouted the country east from Kiowa Creek to the Republican River, but no Indians were found. Wild Bill was leading the men back to Gomer's Mill under the impression that the Indians had gathered at some point for some definite purpose, and so all small bands had been called in.

119

Far up Sand Creek, better known as the Big Sandy, the company rode to the top of a hill. To the east, Indians were seen. The Plains seemed to be covered with them. They were Cheyennes. They attacked the men about three o'clock in the afternoon. Wild Bill and the men had entrenched themselves, and they succeeded in making shelter for the few horses not killed.

They were under attack all the time, and half the force fought while the other half worked. Hickok had a repeating rifle, and there was no lack of ammunition. Milton Garrison, a crack shot, stood beside Wild Bill. They killed many Indians, and finally the savages gave up the attack and retired beyond range. Bill then went down the hill some fifty yards to get in range. Three Indians were sent back to kill Hickok. When about a hundred yards away they began to fire. Bill fell forward, and the Indians believed they had killed him. When the Indians came up he leaped to his feet and killed two of them. The third turned to run, but before he got far Bill killed him, also. Bill was wounded in the leg but not disabled.

Bill knew that it would be impossible for the men to stand siege. They had no water, and they were vastly outnumbered. They could not escape, for few horses were left. It was necessary to seek reinforcements, and Bill determined to go for them himself, knowing the Indians would not attack during the night. He mounted his horse, and at dusk he rode down the mountain slowly and in plain view of the Indians. When they saw that he was trying to escape, they began to close in on him from both sides. It was now a question as to whether he could pass the crucial point before the Indians arrived, but he knew that he must get through the gap, or be captured and tortured to death. As he passed between the two bands they were firing at him, and he was not more than twenty yards from the Indians on his right. A warrior on a fine pony sprang out to kill him. Bill shot the Indian, and as he cleared the gap he uttered a yell of defiance. The Indians pursued him for miles, but he finally escaped, lost in the darkness.

Bill reached the mill about nine o'clock that night. He had ridden forty-five miles in less than three hours! He sent for every settler. He knew that he must be back at the mountain before daylight or the men left there would be massacred. He secured about thirty men, and started back.

It was a rough ride. The trail led over hills, across stretches of Prairie, along divides, through gulches, and down canyons. A few minutes before daylight they neared the mountain. Bill ordered them to yell, every man at the top of his lungs, so that the Indians would be deceived as to their number. The Indians believed a large force was upon them and abandoned the siege. Bill and his men were received with cheers and the joyful manifestations of the men delivered from death. In this daring adventure Bill saved the lives of the thirty-four men. By his action another Arickaree had been avoided. These were the very Indians who met Forsyth a little later.

About the middle of March 1869, Wild Bill was given dispatches to carry from Fort Lyon to Fort Wallace. The Indians were still in their winter camps, and their ponies were unfit for the warpath. Bill anticipated no trouble from them, though he knew that he might find them at any time and place. But such was his confidence that he decided to ride by day and camp by night. On the trail to Fort Wallace nothing out of the ordinary occurred, nor on the return until he neared Fort Lyon.

One day he rode into a bunch of buffalo and killed a fat heifer. He took the tongue and the hump. It was near noon when he reached the Big Sandy near the old Sand Creek battlefield. The bed of the stream was almost dry, but over against a high bank beyond a large bar of gravel there was running water. Bill rode across the bar to let his horse drink. In looking about he saw dry driftwood, and this suggested a fire, broiled buffalo steak, and dinner. He dismounted, gathered wood, made a fire and cooked his fine steaks. He knew that he was not observing his usual caution. He had strapped his trappings to the saddle, and was about to mount when a band of seven Cheyennes appeared on the cut bank above him. They were a chance band of rovers, and had been attracted by the smoke from his fire. In a moment he realized fully the folly of his indiscretion. He was at a disadvantage, but he was disconcerted for a moment only. As the Indians leaped from the bank he began to fire, and four of them tumbled into the stream before their ponies hit the bar. The others rushed upon him and he could not get upon his horse. The leader of the band was mounted on a fine war-pony, and he was armed with a spear having a broad head. This warrior charged Bill, who was prevented from shooting by the rearing of his horse, which he was holding by the bridle gripped at the bit. The Indian struck at him with the spear, and Bill did not entirely escape the plunge. The spear struck him in the right hip. It was a glancing blow, but it inflicted a deep ragged flesh wound. Bill shot this Indian just as another Indian struck at him, missing, the spear striking his rearing horse. As the horse went down Bill shot the warrior. The other Indian was distant a few feet and attempted to ride up the steep bank and escape, but Bill shot him, and he rolled back into the stream.

The fight was over. It had not lasted more than two minutes. There were seven dead Indians, and Bill still wore his own hair. But he was badly hurt. It was with difficulty that he caught the pony of the warrior who had wounded him. He put his saddle and bridle on this pony, gathered up some of the lances or spears, including the one which had

struck him, staunched his wound as best he could, and rode
down the trail for Fort Lyon. He rode with much pain. It
was daylight the next morning when some men sent out to
haul wood found him dragging slowly up the Old Santa Fé
Trail toward the Fort.[2]

The surgeon found the wound a troublesome one, and it
was some time before Bill got around much. He decided that
he would go home and visit his mother while recovering.
Under her care he was soon well and impatient to return to
the Plains. He was just ready to start when he received a
letter from Senator Henry Wilson, of Massachusetts, as
follows:

WASHINGTON, D.C. May 17th, 1869.

James B. Hickok, Esq.:

DEAR SIR: A party consisting of several gentlemen, ladies, and myself,
desire to spend a few weeks in the far west during the warm season, and I
hope it will be our fortune to secure your excellent services as our guide.
I have heard much concerning your wonderful exploits in the West, and
of such a character, too, as commend you highly for efficiency in the
scouting service of the Government. If it be possible for you to accompany
our party as guide some time during the following month, please write me
at once at Willard's Hotel, Washington, indicating what compensation
you will expect, and also from what point in Kansas we had best start on
the tour. I shall leave to you the selection of a pleasant route, as your general
acquaintance with the places of interest between the Missouri river and
the Rocky Mountains better qualifies you for deciding the trip that
promises the most attractions.

Hoping to hear from you at your earliest convenience, I am, Yours truly,

HENRY WILSON

In his reply to Senator Wilson Wild Bill said that his
charges for guiding the expedition would be five hundred
dollars. The party, he said, should leave Fort Hays in June
as in that month the plains were more attractive than in any
other season of the year. Bill immediately set out for Fort
Hays to make arrangements for the trip. Bill was much
surprised to learn that some of the party were women. Mrs.
Wilson was a woman of fine intelligence and of gracious

manner. Before starting she said to him, "Now you are with an unsophisticated crowd of Yankees who know just about as much of the life of the Plains as the person who first discovered there was a man in the moon. I want you to keep a protecting eye on the party, and see that none of them get into trouble."

The date when the party left Fort Hays has not been accurately preserved, but it was about the tenth of June, 1869. The route taken is also in doubt. It is known that the Forks of the Republican and Fort Sedgwick were passed. It was at Cheyenne Canyon, but there is no certainty that it reached the Grand Canyon of the Arkansas, as has been claimed. It came down the Arkansas to Fort Lyon, from which point it came over the old Fort Wallace and Fort Lyon Trail, passing Sand Creek battlefield. From Fort Wallace the party took the usual route to Fort Hays.

The party was gone a little more than a month. Wild Bill had been so efficient that all were delighted with him. Senator Wilson and his guests gave a dinner in honor of Wild Bill in Hays. At the conclusion Senator Wilson arose and complimented Wild Bill very highly, after which he opened a box standing on the table at his right hand and from it took two ivory handled pistols of the finest workmanship. These he presented to Wild Bill as a memento of the wonderful trip over the Plains.

CHAPTER XX · *Wild Bill in 1869 —*
Marshal at Hays

O<small>N</small> <small>HIS</small> return from guiding the party of Senator Wilson, Wild Bill was made the principal peace officer of Hays. Law was lightly regarded; in fact, not regarded at all by a large part of the population. Hays still remained the depot for the trade with Santa Fé. There was a trail from Hays south to the Old Santa Fé Trail. New Mexican products came to Hays in wagons, and an immense quantity of goods was taken back. Large warehouses had been built along the sidings, and these were stored with wool and other shipping from New Mexico, and with goods for trade in that country.

Hays was a reckless town. Its founder left a record of it:

The town was lively but not moral. The streets were lighted from the reflection of the blazing lights of saloons. In addition to dance halls the saloons maintained dances. Women gaudily dressed were striving to hide with ribbons and paint the awful lines which dissipation had drawn upon their faces. These terrible marks were not confined to the women, for many of the men had noses painted cherry red by whiskey. The music was furnished by old-fashioned fiddlers. The rooms were crowded.

. . . .

This scene was duplicated in every saloon and in various dance-halls. Disturbances were frequent in all of them, and these were usually settled with six-shooters. There was no church, and on the Sunday morning which these tourists spent there the chaplain from the fort came over to the town and read the Episcopal morning service from the freight platform. A large crowd assembled, only a few of whom bowed their heads during prayer.

The exact date on which Wild Bill assumed the duties of his office has not been found. At a special election held about the middle of August he was elected sheriff. The vote of

125

this election was canvassed by the county commissioners on the twenty-third of the month. Having been elected to fill a vacancy, his term expired with the next election, and on the second of November he was a candidate to succeed himself, but the town was Democratic in politics, and he was defeated 114 to 89 by Pete Lanahan, Democrat, his deputy.

There was no more lawless town on the border than Hays. In January, three negro soldiers had been taken from the jail at midnight by the people and hanged. Controversies in saloons often ended in death. It frequently happened that as many as five hundred wagon-masters and teamsters were in town at one time. Colonel A. E. Nelson, in command at Fort Hays, sent over a patrol one night in January 1869, and arrested about fifty persons who were engaged in dangerous rowdyism.

Wild Bill patrolled the streets, usually carrying a sawed-off shot-gun and two revolvers, as well as a bowie knife. He went through the saloons and houses of ill fame at night, when dancing was in progress. His presence was enough to guarantee order. It was in one of these dance-halls that Harry Young, author of *Hard Knocks*, met Bill. He had become enamored of a girl with whom he danced; and spent nearly forty dollars in entertaining her. Wild Bill noted the extravagance of this youth, who stood on the sidewalk next morning deliberating as to what he should do with his remaining dollar and a half. Bill touched him on the shoulder and inquired where he came from. He told the boy that he had observed him the night before and gave him some wholesome advice. He then asked the boy if he could drive a six-mule team. He could not. Bill said he could learn, and taking him into a saloon, taught him to tie a government hamestring. The following morning Bill took the boy to Fort Hays and introduced him to the corral boss, requesting that he be put to work. The boss put the same question which

[MAIN STREET, HAYS CITY, FROM AN OLD PRINT]

Bill had asked. Could he drive a six-mule team? Bill replied, "Yes," not waiting for the boy to answer. The boss threw a mule collar on the ground and told him to tie the hames. He tied the knot correctly. The boss said to Bill, "You certainly drilled him well!" However, it was agreed that the boy should be given a chance. In a day or two Bill went out to see how his protégé was progressing and was surprised to find that he was already driving a six-mule team. He rode along with the boy for a while, giving him instructions in driving, telling him that these suggestions were the result of his experience in driving teams of all descriptions over the Old Santa Fé Trail. This boy worked at the fort for six months.

The founder of Hays City met Wild Bill and Buffalo Bill on the day he was prepared to depart for his tour of the prairies. In his observations he notes that the name Wild Bill had become a household word to the residents of the Kansas frontier. He states that Bill was quiet and gentlemanly, and by no means the bad man he had expected to see. He found that Bill carried two pistols, with one of which he had killed a man only a few days before.

Jim Curry was one of the notorious characters at Hays. He had been a locomotive engineer on the Kansas Pacific Railroad. While his name is not on the roll, there is reason to believe that he was one of the scouts with Forsyth at the battle of the Arickaree. He was a reckless and dangerous man and the enemy of Wild Bill by instinct. C. J. Bascom of Ellis, Kansas, published an article in the *Kansas City Star* June 15, 1913, entitled "Wild Bill Days in Kansas." He described this incident.

A short time after Wild Bill was made marshal of Hays, Curry started his saloon and restaurant. As the proprietor of this institution he was under the constant surveillance of Wild Bill. One day Bascom went into his saloon to get his lunch and was invited by Curry to take a walk. They went to the most famous saloon ever established in Hays, or in fact, in any town along the Kansas Pacific. The proprietor of this saloon was Tommy Drum, a Scotchman, a man always on the square and one who required no portion of the eternal vigilance bestowed by Wild Bill. Bascom and Curry found Wild Bill playing cards in Drum's saloon, sitting with his back to the door, but so far back that he anticipated no trouble from the position. But his judgment was at fault.

Curry slipped up behind and pressed his cocked revolver against his head, saying, "Now, you son of a gun! I've got you!" Bill did not move a muscle. He showed no concern. He realized his danger but he said in a casual way, "Jim, you would not murder a man without giving him a show!" Jim replied, "I'll give you the same show you would give me, you long-haired tough!" Every one present knew the peril in which Bill stood, and the suspense was awful. Tommy Drum's oath was "By the boot!" He was running about the saloon in great perturbation exclaiming "By the boot!" "By the boot!" Bill was really the only cool, self-contained man in the room, and remarked "Jim, let us settle this feud. How would a bottle of champagne all around do?" The manner in which Bill had taken the whole incident, and the unconcern with which he made this remark relieved the tension, and all burst out laughing. Tommy Drum opened a pint bottle of champagne for every one present. Curry and Bill shook hands and the feud between them was over.

There was in Hays a one-armed man who was a terror when drunk. He went into Chris Riley's saloon and raised a disturbance. Bill went in and warned him to quiet down and behave himself. He turned on Bill and said, "Yes, you blankety blank bee-hunter, you! You can bluff me when I ain't armed, but if I had a gun I'd show you!" Instantly Bill drew one of his pistols, placed it on the counter and quietly remarked, "There's your gun, pardner. What will you do with it?" The one-armed man snatched up the gun and leveled it at Bill's heart. Before he could shoot Bill struck him with his fist on the jaw and sent him unconscious to the floor. He turned to his friend, Hill P. Wilson, later Assistant Secretary of State, who was standing by, and said, "And now they will say Wild Bill struck a cripple. But I had to, didn't I, Hill, or else kill him?" To which Hill and all present assented.

Bascom gives this incident of Bill's enforcement of order at Hays:

Bill was ruling the town with an iron hand. It was something unusual and unexpected. The bad men were puzzled. They did not know just what to think nor how long this rule would last. Bill had not been tried out in the capacity of peace officer in that vicinity. Two soldiers met him one day at Kruger's corner. They stopped him, and one of them said, "So you are the long-haired son of a gun that *Harper's Magazine* talks so much about. I enlisted for the purpose of coming out here and doing you up." He drew his revolver, and the other man stood by to help. Before he could shoot Bill drew, fired, and killed them both. The man who had challenged Bill was a son of one Estes, of the firm of Wilson, Estes, and Fairchild, foundrymen at Leavenworth.

A notable incident in the administration of Wild Bill as city marshal of Hays was the killing of Jack, or as some call him Sam, Strawhan. The trouble began at Ellsworth, although he was a resident of Hays. He was a desperado and a bully. He had killed a number of men, which fact he frequently proclaimed. Wild Bill was in Ellsworth on official business. Strawhan at that time became intoxicated to the point where he wanted to kill. Two or three of his associates were with him, and they started out to clean up the town of Ellsworth.

One Kingsbury, the redoubtable Captain quoted so often by Buel and on whom rest so many of his statements and mis-statements, was sheriff of Ellsworth County. He summoned all the bystanders to assist in arresting the ruffians. Among those upon whom he called for assistance was Wild Bill, under whose direction the gang was arrested. At that time there was no jail in Ellsworth. Strawhan became very violent. To confine him they tied him to a post. He was kept in that position until he became sober and agreed to leave town. But he carried resentment against the men who had subdued him, and swore that he would kill Kingsbury, his deputy—one Whitney, and Wild Bill.

In a few days after his return to Hays he went into Tommy Drum's saloon. Wild Bill was there. He saw Strawhan the moment he stepped in but pretended not to see him. Straw-

han must have believed that his entrance had been unnoticed and that Bill was off his guard. He raised his pistol
and was about to fire. Bill then drew his pistol and fired,
striking Strawhan in the right eye, killing him instantly.
Bill invited everyone to take a drink and had the coroner
sent for. The coroner arrived in a few minutes, took the
testimony of the crowd, and his jury acquitted Bill without
retiring to deliberate. It was said that the town brass-band
was followed by a large procession when it went to serenade
Bill that night. The account of this affair given by Buffalo
Bill in an interview published in the *Chicago Inter-Ocean* is
quite different. In some accounts of this matter it is said
that Bill did not turn at all, but kept his face to the bar.
Looking into the mirror he fired over his shoulder, his bullet
striking Strawhan in the center of his forehead, killing him
instantly. This may very possibly be true.

Another incident which occurred at Hays gained wide
currency. Later various points were given as the place at
which this happened, among them Abilene and Ellsworth.
McCoy, who employed Bill as marshal of Abilene, says it
was in that town. Colonel Cody placed it at Hays. That the
incident is genuine there is no question, and it illustrates the
poise, coolness, and quick-thinking of Wild Bill. The name
of the opponent has not been preserved. A man had nursed
a grudge against Wild Bill and sworn to kill him. He dared
not face Bill in the open and so he lay in ambush in a dark
doorway. When Bill came along the man stepped out with
a drawn pistol and said, "I've got you now, Wild Bill! I'm
going to kill you and I'll give you one minute to pray."
"Well," said Bill, with an easy smile, "It does look like the
jig's up." Then Bill looked beyond his antagonist and said,
"Don't hit him, Andy!" Instinctively the man wheeled to
see who was in his rear. He gazed into the empty space.
There was no one behind him. When he turned he looked into

the muzzle of Wild Bill's pistol-barrel—and there was another candidate for Boot Hill.

Much of the disorder at Hays was caused by the troops from the fort. Many of them were desperate characters and indulged in every kind of dissipation. They would come into Hays at nightfall, shoot in the streets, shoot up the saloons, break the furniture, kill people, and hurry back to the fort. These characteristics in some instances attached to the officers. Custer's brother, Tom, who was an officer in the Seventh Cavalry, would ride through the town at breakneck speed yelling like a Comanche and shooting with both hands. He would ride into the saloons, shoot them up and ride out. He thought his military connection made him immune from arrest by civil authority. On one occasion he rode into a billiard hall at night and tried to force his horse to jump upon the billiard tables. The horse would not perform this act, and Custer shot and killed him in the billiard hall.

Wild Bill arrested Custer. Custer had boasted that he would never submit to an arrest, but when he saw that Wild Bill would kill him if he did not submit he went quietly enough. Bill took him before the police judge where he was heavily fined.

This action of Wild Bill angered and humiliated Tom Custer. He selected three reckless and desperate ruffians and accompanied them into town with the understanding that they would kill Wild Bill. It was planned that one soldier would leap upon his back and force him over, while another was to pinion his arms. The third man was then to kill him.

Bill was found in a small saloon so imperfectly lighted and full of tobacco smoke that it was almost impossible to distinguish one person from another. This enabled them to approach him. One powerful soldier leaped upon him, bearing him over, and the second clasped him round, to pinion his arms. Bill wrested one arm free. With his left hand Bill drew his pistol and fired backward over his shoulder at the man forcing him down. The soldier fell from Bill's back a dead man. In a minute Bill was erect. He shot the soldier who was waiting in front of him with drawn pistol. Then he fired over his shoulder and killed the man who had pinioned his arms and who had his pistol drawn. Custer had brought a number of soldiers who were to aid these select three if they should fail. But the citizens intervened and they were driven from the town, uttering threats and swearing vengeance.

Captain Jack Crawford described the above incident in his lectures. As he told it there were but two men, and he acted the scene. This is probably the most famous incident of coolness, nerve and skill in shooting the world has known. Crawford said that the possibility of the act had been denied. But to vindicate the prowess of his old-time friend and comrade he had practised the movement until he knew it could be done. And he demonstrated how. So quickly did he move that the two reports of his pistol could not be distinguished. And he said that he was slow and only a bungler as compared to Wild Bill.

When Tom Custer and his ruffians had been driven out of town, the people went to Bill and urged him to leave Hays until the matter quieted down. Bill refused to go. He said he would be called a coward. His friends said it was not cowardice—that he could not successfully fight the whole Seventh Cavalry, something he would have to do if he remained.

John W. McDanield, founder of Bonner Springs, was the pioneer locomotive engineer of the Kansas Pacific. He was in Hays that night. He was Bill's friend, having carried him back and forth over the road since 1866. He went to Bill to make a last appeal. It was just before he had to pull out with a freight-train for Kansas City. He finally prevailed on Bill to go with him. They went down to the train, and McDanield

pulled out. He has often told the author that he made passenger time with that freight for a few miles, for as they
boarded the engine a body of men could be seen riding in
from the fort.

The exact date of this event has not been preserved, but
Bill was at Hays as late as December 21, 1869, on which date
a Topeka paper mentions that he had shipped a whole
buffalo to the Topeka House, Topeka. John W. McDanield
said he brought Wild Bill down from Hays about the first of
January 1870, but could not fix an exact date. It must have
been New Year's Day 1870, and Tom Custer must have
been ending the holidays with a burst of deviltry and rowdyism.

Quotations from the *Topeka Commonwealth* in 1869 follow: November 18—Sheriff Hickok, of Ellis County, yclept,
in many a well-known story of border-life "Wild Bill," is in
town, registered at the Topeka House. Long may he be at
Hays.

> Shake his ambrosial locks and give the nod,
> The stamp of fate, the sanction of a god!"

December 9—Hays City under the guardian care of "Wild
Bill" is quiet and doing well.

December 21—Jas. B. Hickok, *alias* Wild Bill, sent a whole
buffalo to McNeelin yesterday, from Hays City. Mac served
up buffalo roasts and steaks today with the usual et ceteras.

CHAPTER XXI · *Wild Bill in Topeka, Winter 1869-70*

WILD BILL left the freight train at Ellsworth, remained a day or two with friends there and later went on to Kansas City. He decided not to do much work in the winter of 1869–70. A vacation after so many strenuous years would not be amiss. He would spend the winter in Topeka. The legislature would be in session and many of his old friends of the army and Plains days would be in town. Buffalo Bill had brought Mrs. Cody to Topeka for the winter, and he was to be there much of the time himself. Topeka was then nothing more than a frontier town, full of saloons and gambling houses, a high-pressure town of board shanties and board sidewalks. A few flagstone walks were to be found on Kansas Avenue. There was no paving in town, and no sewers.

Wild Bill came to Topeka about the first of January 1870, probably in time for the opening session of the legislature. His old-time friend and comrade, Colonel H. C. Lindsay, was then a deputy sheriff, but he was still operating his livery stable and sales stables.

Bill spent much time with Colonel Lindsay. He enjoyed standing about the corrals where the horses were gathered. Many men congregated there, to gossip, spin yarns, and "talk horse." Bill also frequented the sheriff's office. He often went on rounds of inspection of saloons and dance-halls with the marshal. On one of these trips, in a saloon in the basement of the building at Sixth and Kansas Avenue, Bill found

134

[KANSAS AVENUE, TOPEKA, IN WILD BILL'S TIME]

a citizen so bad that he had forced him to leave Hays. The "bad" man was in his cups. He had heard that Bill had left Hays because of his affair with the Seventh Cavalry, and thought he might safely taunt him now.

"You ran me out of Hays," he said, "I might as well have stayed on. I think I'll run you out of Topeka." Drawing his pistol, he said to Bill: "Now, you git———."

That was as far as he went. Bill rapped him over the head with a revolver. When the "bad" man picked himself up Bill said to him:

"You have time to make the K.P. train to Kansas City. Go to Lindsay's livery barn and have one of his drivers take you to the station and tell the driver to report to me when he returns. And if I ever see you in Kansas again, I'll kill you. Now, move." And Bill helped him out with a swift kick. In an hour the driver reported to Bill that the passenger he had taken to the depot had been eager to board the train and depart.

Next morning Bill voluntarily appeared before Police Judge Holmes and told of the incident. He said he had come in to plead guilty and pay his fine. The judge said Bill had only done the proper thing. But Bill insisted and the Judge fined him five dollars, which he promptly paid. The notice of the incident in the morning paper was:

Wild Bill was fined $5.00 and costs yesterday for punching the head of some unfortunate mortal, whose name we did not learn.

Here is the story of a young man who "got the drop" on Wild Bill—and lived to tell of it. Bill and a number of friends were in a poker game at the Topeka house. A very young man had "set in" at the game. At its close Wild Bill had won. As he raked in the stakes, the young man suddenly and unexpectedly drew his revolver, shoved it against Bill's breast and shouted "Hands up!" Bill promptly responded. His hands went up. The young man picked up the winnings, saying that *he* had won, and started to back out of the room. The other players were excited, but Bill was not disturbed. He said, quietly, "Come back here, son, and listen to me. You're all right, but you're mistaken. I'm sure you think you won the game but you've got a lot to learn about poker. Sit down, and let me tell you about it."

The young man came back to the table, and Bill patiently went over the game with him. He saw that he had been wrong. Bill said, "I don't hold your gun-play against you. You may have the money. I'll make you a present of it—with this advice. In the future, be careful to know the game you play. And never flash a gun unless you have to, to defend yourself. And—you've got a lot to learn. Now, let's all have a drink."

That winter George M. Stone, an artist, living now in Topeka, saw Wild Bill on Kansas Avenue about Fifth Street, with Buffalo Bill. Buffalo Bill took his hat and spun it up into the air. Wild Bill shot an evenly spaced row of holes along the outside of the rim as it was falling, and before it touched the ground.

In this same year, Charles LeTourette ran a sample room and gambling house near the corner of Sixth and Kansas Avenue. William Young and William Marshall were the most noted gamblers in Topeka at that time—professional gamblers. One day Young, Marshall, Wild Bill, and LaTourette were driving on Kansas Avenue in a new buggy. At Third and Kansas Avenue the team reared, broke their harness, and ran away. Wild Bill jumped over the dash board, walked out on the tongue, grabbed the horses by their heads and stopped them. It was a daring and dangerous feat.

J. L. Marshall often saw Wild Bill in Atchison, Kansas. Bill would show him how to shoot—under his arm or over his shoulder. Marshall said Bill was a dead shot and as quick as a flash—never took aim.

[TOPEKA IN THE EARLY DAYS—FROM A PHOTOGRAPH]

Marshall's father was a plasterer. Bill was sometimes at a house they were plastering. One day Marshall asked him the time. Bill stepped to the door, looked at the sun and said it was a quarter to three o'clock. Marshall was surprised and said, "Why did you go and look out to find the time? You have a watch."

"I went to look at the sun," said Bill. "I always tell the time by the sun, or moon or stars. I have no use for a watch except in cloudy weather and not much then, but I carry one." Young Marshall was curious to know if he had given the time correctly and consulted a clock: Bill was right.

CHAPTER XXII · *Cowboys and Cowboy Life*

THE story of the cowboy is the great saga of the Southwest. Men, high-spirited and gay, living the lusty heyday of their youth joyously, recklessly. For background the rolling spread of prairie and Plain, wind-swept and sky-circled. And stretching long gray ribands, drawn taut across the vast tableland, the cattle-trails, reaching up out of Texas, across wild Indian lands, into Kansas. Literally, the highways of the Empire Builders.

Cattle! Trails! Prosaic words! How little suggestive of any vision or emotion. And yet traffic in cattle over the Southwestern Plains, sprung deep-rooted, from the very soil of romance. The Texas Longhorn himself bore the blood of cattle that had grazed the hills and meadows of Spain centuries before Coronado came seeking Quivira.

When Texas was a Mexican province one hundred thousand head of Spanish cattle were imported. But under the Spaniard the commerce in cattle never developed into a thing of any scope. However, the cattle quickly adapted themselves to the new environment, and as the grass, the water, and the climate were all ideal for their existence, they increased enormously. They were restless, wild creatures, sleek, big-eyed, with an amazing width of horns. They were fleet, wiry, and they were gifted with the courage of demons.

During the years of the Civil War, they remained practically unmolested. Neither the North nor the South, however great their need, could reach them. There was no market. War closed the way to the North and in their thorny fastness,

138

these cattle could not be reached by the famishing Confederacy. By the close of the Civil War there were well over three and one-half millions of the longhorns. Texas possessed enormous wealth, and yet, because of lack of marketing facilities, poverty stalked the fattest pastures on which the sun every had shone.

The ending of the Civil War released numberless young men. Many of them turned with zest to the cattle-country of the Southwest for that adventure and excitement they ardently demanded of life. These men sought a market, a way to realize on their living grazing resources. In 1865 and 1866 some of the owners resolved to try for northern markets. Accordingly, in the summer of 1866, a colossal herd of two hundred and seventy thousand head was gathered in Northeast Texas, to be driven through Missouri.

No regular trail had been mapped out. But the great herd was started north on its long journey over plain and hill and river. Indians threatened and stole. Bandits ran off small bunches. Outlaws levied outrageous taxes for the privilege of passing through, and then stampeded cattle and tortured drivers. Spanish fever caused great loss. When the herd finally reached Missouri it was sadly depleted and was in poor condition. The year's work had produced no profit; in fact, there was a loss.

This venture only emphasized the necessity for a market which could be reached with safety and dispatch. The cattlemen were more determined than ever to find it. Then out of a clear sky dropped Joseph G. McCoy. He was a young ex-soldier—a man who saw in the cattle-business a way of satisfying his need for action and profit. He brought to bear on the subject all his energy and intelligence. McCoy conceived the idea of finding and marking a definite trail, to be followed by all the Texas drovers up to a single shipping-point. This was to be the point to which the Kansas Pacific

Railroad should then have been completed. The story of his efforts, his discouragements, and his final victory is a tale of action and courage.

Abilene, at that time thirty miles beyond the terminus of the Kansas Pacific, was one hundred and sixty-five miles from Kansas City, the great shipping point from which the South might reach the East. McCoy at last induced the Kansas Pacific to extend its line to Abilene and install a switch for a hundred cars. So skeptical did the railroad men remain that they used old discarded ties and insisted that a switch for twenty cars was really more than would be needed.

McCoy himself constructed yards and loading facilities and installed scales. The prairie about Abilene presented ideal grazing grounds for the cattle awaiting shipment.

These preparations completed, McCoy sent a man with a thorough knowledge of the geography of the Southwest as a messenger to bear the intelligence of what had been accomplished at Abilene for the Texas stockmen. He rode from one great herd to another, with the all-absorbing topic of Abilene, the new shipping point and outlet for the Great Southwest at the terminus of the Kansas Pacific for his theme. He carried information about the best route, maps to show its location, and plans for saving time and distance. The stockmen were inclined to regard this messenger with skepticism. They suspected a trap of some sort, and so a great many were surly and unresponsive.

However a herd of two thousand head was sent out by a Mr. Thompson. In the Indian nation these cattle were sold to Smith, McCord, and Chandler, who drove them safely through to Abilene. They formed the vanguard of an immense throng. The trail they broke was to harden into a rock-like pavement under the thundering hoofs of mighty herds.

The first shipment from Abilene was made September 5, 1867. There was a celebration, with a special train of Illinois stock-dealers, who had come on to witness the beginning of the movement, as guests of honor. Thirty-six thousand head of cattle were shipped from Abilene the first season. In spite of loss from Indians and floods, there was a profit shown at the close of the year. The Texas drovers were convinced and began to make great plans for the following season. In 1868, seventy-five thousand head were shipped. In 1869, one hundred and sixty thousand head of cattle came sweeping up in a great horned army from the Southwest and were entrained for market at Abilene.

And by this time there were definitely marked and worn Trails. The most famous of them all was the "Chisholm Trail." It ran as follows:

Up through Texas by many branches to the Red River, at the north boundary of Montague County, at Red River Station Crossing near the mouth of Salt Creek (half a mile above, and half a mile below the mouth of Fleetwood), then following Fleetwood Creek to its head. Thence to Wild Horse Creek. From there to a point west of Signal Mountain and across the Washita at Elm Springs, and north to the Canadian River. Thence it followed Kingfisher Creek to the Cimarron. It touched the heads of Black Bear and Bluff Creeks, then the Salt Fork of the Arkansas. It entered Kansas at Caldwell, crossed the Arkansas at Wichita, and ran northeast over the divide between the Smoky Hill and the Arkansas, straight to Abilene.

In time the Chisholm trail came to be a hard-packed, barebeaten highway two hundred to four hundred yards in width and six hundred miles long. There were detours, of course, used in time of flood or drouth or Indian uprising. Literally worn down into the earth by the restless hoofs of the countless numbers that traveled that grievous journey to death,

it ran between low banks. It was marked at intervals by
great circular "bedding grounds," still to be seen in many
places. Beside the trail whitened the bones of many cattle.
And, occasionally, a little wooden cross marked the grave
of some striken cowboy, buried on the lone prairie.

There were other trails. The Old Shawnee Trail, which led
to Baxter Springs, was much used. Between it and the Chisholm Trail ran the West Shawnee, or Middle Trail. This
latter ended at Junction City, which was becoming another
important shipping point. There was also the Western
Chisholm, usually written "Chisum," which led into Wyoming and Montana. In time the Chisholm Trail was surveyed, straightened, made more direct, and so a further
time-saving was effected.

The business of driving and shipping cattle was becoming
of mammoth proportions. From Abilene alone, in 1870, were
shipped three hundred thousand head of cattle. In 1871, one
million head were shipped east, and of these, six hundred
thousand were shipped from Abilene. Texas cattle poured
in a great flood into Eastern markets. Sometimes, so close
together ran the great herds on the trail during the months
of July, August, and September, that the leaders of one almost trod on the heels of another.

Around Abilene the scene was inspiring: sleek, resting
herds, grazing contentedly, as far as the eye could see. Camps
and "cavie yards" here and there. Cowboys, one watchful
eye on the longhorns, smoking and loafing in their saddles.
Prosperity and wealth spread in a great circle over the
prairie around the town.

The cowboys were picturesque and stirring figures on the
Great Plains. They had a life and traits in common, but in-
dividually they came from the four ends of the world and
differed in personality, race, creed, and general standards of
life. The boys from the armies of the North and the South,

brave, reckless, ardent young fellows with an honest outlook and few illusions left on life. Roughs and border bad men, drifters, always trouble-makers wherever found! Easterners, educated and clever, looking for a chance to gain health or money! Soft-voiced Californians, whose drawling speech and sleepy movements betrayed their Southern origin and belied their energy, courage, and lightning action when occasion demanded. Spaniards, some few Indians, many half-breeds, and more Mexicans. Any and every man eager and willing to work and face death and the hardships of cowboy life.

No one every saw a real cowboy without his lariat. He became expert in its use and his pony was usually as expert as himself. When the prey was caught, the pony braced himself to hold a tight rope. It was no trick at all to throw a heavy steer. Each unbranded animal had to be roped, thrown, and held until branded.

The cowboy seldom slept under a roof or in a bed. He loved danger and he hated work. He never walked anywhere that his pony could carry him. And indeed in this he was wise, for an unmounted man had no chance for his life among the longhorns. The cattle accorded fear and respect to a man on a pony. But they trampled him to death if he went among them on foot.

The cowboy wore a wide-brimmed, tall-crowned sombrero. This kept the glare of the sun from his eyes. And there were developed soon, huge shaggy chaps to protect his legs from rain and from the stiff, thorny scrub through which he often rode. He gloried in an ornamented belt supporting a couple of "six-guns" and their necessary ammunition. Huge silver spurs attached to the heels of his boots clinked as he walked or danced. The heels of these same boots were high, both from vanity and utility. They served to brace him by dragging deep into the earth as he held the rope of a captured pony. A flaming handkerchief knotted at the back of his neck added a gaudy note to the general scheme. It was a prided ornament and of use to wipe the perspiration from his eyes. Add to this picture an aversion to soap and a fear, amounting almost to an obsession, of water, taken either internally or as applied externally. Long hair and unshaven visages added to the general ensemble. Flannel shirts and fleas were common.

On the range the cowboys lived in little groups in tents or cabins. On the trail they camped near the cattle on their bedding ground. There were very few tents. Most of the men slept rolled in blankets on the ground around the fire or under the "chuck wagons." A man whom a rainstorm or wet blankets could keep awake was regarded as effeminate and a menace to real manhood.

A chuck-wagon and a cook were two high lights in the long march. The cook, aware of his importance, and as temperamental as any other artist, demanded and always commanded respectful treatment. He was seldom the victim of the incessant practical jokes that helped to divert the cowboys, for his mode of revenge might include scalding water or a week of soggy leaden biscuits. But his assistant rarely escaped a full life—one precarious and brimming with fervid action. The usual fare consisted of bacon or salt pork, beans, corn-bread or biscuits, and coffee. No cowboy considered a meal successful unless washed down with at least a scalding quart of the liquid lye he fondly called coffee. "Put 'er back and let 'er bile a while longer," was a frequent request when the inky fluid had been steaming only half an hour or so. Occasionally there was fresh beef, and sometimes potatoes and onions were on the menu. The latter vegetable was always greeted with deep and fervent joy. And no cowboy needed to be coaxed at mealtime. The longed-for howl of "Come and get it," usually resulted in near riot. Niceties of table manners had been discarded along with napkins and forks, but kind Nature furnished each man with ten fingers and the boss donated him a tin plate. Some of the boys used a jack-knife. The festivities were brief but fervent.

The wages of the cowboy ranged from fourteen to twenty-five dollars a month. Mexicans were satisfied with about twelve dollars. Much of his money went for the tobacco that helped to while away the long hours of monotonous riding, and the dragging midnight hours of "riding herd." This tobacco, and the practical jokes in which he took such enor-mous pleasure, the joshing and songs and stories—the latter usually none too nice—constituted his day-by-day recrea-tions. Occasionally some musical individual "toted" a jews'-harp or a fiddle in his "war bag" wherewith he fed his yearn-ing soul.

The "war bag" consisted of anything from a flour sack to a battered satchel, held his more intimate personal belong-ings—extra shirt and socks and neckerchief, tobacco, pic-tures of the home-folks, of his girl, combs and dime-novels, a miscellany of small possessions. The regulation equipment which he himself furnished consisted of blankets, slicker, a "tarp" of canvas for a bedding-roll, saddle-blankets, bridle, and saddle. These two latter were his pride and on them he proudly lavished silver mountings and ornaments and braided leather.

The outfit for which he worked furnished the ponies. The boys were not encouraged to own their mounts. The ponies were usually wiry, half-tamed broncos, and from six to ten were provided for each man's use. They, too, like the cattle, were branded with their owner's mark. They were alert and quick to act, and trained to brace and hold a taut rope on a fighting, struggling steer. Very often they formed a dog-like attachment for some particular man. And most of the boys, lonely for an affection which they would loudly have denied needing, manifested an extravagant attachment for some one pony. The cowboy was apt to grow boastful over the accomplishments and abilities of this pony, and turned a lenient eye on such trifles as bucking, biting, and kicking.

The ponies were generally named by the "breaker," and often their titles were suggested by some individual trait or appearance. "Cannon Ball," "Big Enough," "Rattler," "Slippers," "Jesse James," "Monte," "Few Brains," "Apron Face," "Butterbeans," "Lightning," "Julius Caesar," "Pudding Foot"—these are specimens of the nomenclature.

Before the cattle were started on their long march they were rounded up and given a "road brand." This was to facilitate speedy identification in case of stampede or at the shipping yards. Previous to this time the cattle had been untouched by human hand since their first branding, four years before.

As any unbranded stray, known as "maverick," was the property of the man on whose land it was found, many herds received large additions from this source. And as some of the great cattle barons did not live on their holdings and depended on the honesty of their foreman, there were opportunities for a dishonest man to acquire great wealth—unless he was so unfortunate as to be found out and invited for the chief guest at a necktie-party.

Once ready for the road, the herd was started. The cowboys rode at intervals beside them. There were always some steers who took the lead, day after day, and others who as unvaryingly lagged behind.

The herd was allowed to graze in the morning. About noon it was rounded up and urged along until twilight. Again it was allowed to graze. About nightfall the cowboys gathered it into a great group by riding around it in a steadily lessening circle. Now was the time when the cowboy usually began to sing. This was done to tranquilize the cattle, so that they would lie down. Any monotonous chant was used at first.

Hymns were favorites. It was no uncommon thing to see some villainous-looking ruffian droning camp-meeting favorites for the benefit of the cattle. Later, songs reflecting lives and thoughts of the cowboys themselves developed.

At midnight the herd always stirred, got up, and turned around. This was the time most dreaded by the cowboys, for it often ended in a stampede. Some trifle, the howl of a coyote, the sudden flame of the campfire, a flash of lightning, the hysterical fear of a leader-steer—any little thing might start a wild, reckless flight. Insane with fright, the cattle would race blindly over a cliff, or into any other certain death.

Now was the time when the cowboys rose to their supreme height. At first it was hard work even to keep up with the cattle. But there were always some ponies fleeter than the cattle, and gradually, as they reached the head of the mad column, the men began to force the leaders to turn. It was dangerous work, riding at terrific speed over unknown ground, with the chance that the pony might plunge down an embankment, tear through a bunch of cat-claw, go over a cliff, or step in a gopher-hole and throw his rider. And woe to the man whose pony had stumbled. There was no mercy in those wild, trampling hoofs. Death often claimed a victim from the stampede.

By constant pushing of the leaders, the herd was compelled at last to run in a great circle. The circle was steadily lessened and made more compact. This rotary slowing down was known as "milling." And now again the cowboy sang lustily and loudly. "The Dying Cowboy," "Mustang Gray," "California Joe," "The Dreary Black Hills"—these and others, were chanted on many a night till dawn dimmed the stars.

When drouth sucked up the streams and dried the water-holes the cattle suffered, and their distressed bellowing bore a note akin to that of human despair. Hour after hour of thirst

and dust and heat! The long marching column took on the
character of a tortured procession of the damned. The trip
from Texas to Abilene required from forty to one hundred
days—circumstances governing the time.

And at his journey's end the cowboy found the crude little
shipping town,—at first an aimless huddle of flimsy wooden
boxes, dropped grotesquely on the prairies. It lay, a few
straggling, crooked streets of unpainted pine buildings ad-
joining the depot and the stock yards. But the jeweled lights
of New York mean no more to the traveler of today than the
feeble lamp and candle gleams of the crude new Abilene
meant to the cowboy. And there is small doubt that Abilene
of the late sixties and early seventies could have given
Sodom and Gomorrah pointers on murder and lust and general corruption. For all those harpies who prey on humanity
flocked to the cattle towns. Crooked gamblers, three-card
monte men, sharpers, thieves, murderers, women of the
streets, all these abounded there. Hash-houses, saloons,
dance-halls, dives, lined the streets. They had fancy names
such as "The Mint," "The Alamo," "The Gold Room,"
"The Bull's Head," "The Sidetrack," "The Do-Drop-In."
The town was a trap baited with cards and drink and music
and the tawdry silks of harlots.

And to it, the cowboy came for his one surcease from a
year of loneliness. The reaction carried him far beyond the
line of normal life. Is it a wonder that he was easy prey?
or that a brave marshal was needed to protect him from the
town—and the town from him? Such a man was Wild Bill.
Of him it was said: "Occasionally a marshal was found like
James Hickok, the original Wild Bill, who could rule Abilene
at its worst period because he was quicker with his revolver
and more daring than any of the cowboys themselves."

The first thing on the cowboy's program was the paying
off. And sometimes it was not a matter easily adjusted to the

[FRONT STREET, DODGE CITY, FROM AN OLD PRINT]

satisfaction of both boss and man. One cowboy, bursting
into dolorous melody, sadly sings—

> I went to the boss to draw my roll,
> And he had it all figured out.
> I was nine dollars in the hole.

But usually there was a more amiable adjustment, after
which the cowboy made a hurried visit to the barber. Here
some six months' growth of hair and whiskers was subjugated
and he issued forth to delve into the gorgeous apparel of
some Jew clothing store. New clothes added to his high
spirits. He was now ready for his recreations, and his hilarity
was mounting steadily. Abrupt yells and shrieks, denoting
felicity, issued from his throat as his pony tore madly along
the streets. Sometimes in drunken exuberance, he "shot up"
the town and abruptly ended his vacation in the calaboose.
His temporarily more discreet companions crowded saloons
and dance-halls and dives. Raucous music issued from battered pianos, and rickety buildings shook and trembled as
the cowboy and his partner treaded the "light measure."

The cowboy entered the dance-hall clad in his sombrero,
spurs, and pistols. He did not remove his hat but tipped it at
a sharp angle. He was not versed in the finer forms of dancing. His experience in that line had been gained in log cabins
of the frontier in the country hoe-down. At the end of the
dance the cowboy waltzed to the bar and treated his partner,
imbibing deeply himself.

Sometimes quarrels would ensue, and insults would be
hurled. As many as six cowboys have been killed in a dance-
house in such a brawl. Occasionally a war would break out
between dance-houses and saloons. The crowd at one place
would start for that at another, a battle would ensue, and
result in the death of numerous characters who could well be
spared. Frequently, some cowboy against whom nothing
could be said but that he was in bad company, lost his life.

The authorities took no note of what occurred in these "wars." There was rarely any possibility of finding who was at fault or who had killed any particular man.

There is much excuse for cowboy conduct. Miles away from home, he lived half-forgotten by his "folks," lonely, perhaps jilted and forsaken by some girl who tired of waiting for him.

The prairie sunset painted the skies with glorious streamers and banners of gold and jade and scarlet. The moon rose and floated in liquid silver high above the Plains. Far below the tiny town pulsated and swayed with life and revelry. Down there the moonlight was paled by the flaring windows of the saloons; the quiet of the night was torn and disturbed by the beat and throb of sensual and reckless music.

But a few miles outside the little circle were peace and silence and countless stars shining in the blue vaults of heaven.

The cattle loaded, his money spent, his appetite jaded, and his disposition "soured," the cowboy turned his back on Abilene and returned to the range for another year of toil.

*   *   *

The big year for the cattle business was 1871. It marked the climax of production and shipping and prices. The year 1872 found business steadily on the down grade. Though there were extensive drives for many years after, the business never again attained the huge proportions of 1871. Blizzards and ice-bound pastures, Spanish fever, and falling prices all worked together to play havoc. Of the output of 1872, three hundred thousand head of cattle remained unsold, and during the following winter most of them died. The boom at Abilene collapsed in 1873.

Ellsworth, forty miles further west, became the Kansas Pacific Railroad shipping-point. The Atchison, Topeka, and

Santa Fé ignored Abilene and established shipping-points of its own—Newton and other places. And the railroads began reaching down into Northern Texas, so that it was not necessary to drive cattle into Kansas to ship them to market.

But even as late as 1891 an occasional herd came swinging up over the old Chisholm Trail into Abilene.

It was a great life while it lasted. But the day of the cowboy and the cowboy town has passed. They have joined the long procession of ghosts in which every man and every period ultimately takes its appointed place.

But standing at some point by the side of the old Chisholm Trail one can re-vision the marching column, can hear again the rumbling tread of the great herds, can feel the earth quiver under their passing feet. And perhaps, on some still starlight night, out under the high-flung arch of the Milky Way, one can sense the presence of some shadowy cowboy "Riding Herd" and hear again his song.

> Oh say, little dogies,[1] when you going to lay down
>   And quit this forever shifting around?
> My limbs are weary, my seat is sore,
>   Oh lay down, dogies, like you've laid down before—
> Lay down, little dogies, lay down.
>
> Oh lay still, dogies, since you have laid down,
>   Stretch away out on the big open ground;
> Snore loud, little dogies, and drown the wild sound
>   That will go away when the day rolls around—
> Lay still, little dogies, lay still.

---

[1] An affectionate and provincial name for cattle.

CHAPTER XXIII · *Wild Bill—Marshal of Abilene*

WHEN McCoy decided on Abilene as the future shipping point for cattle, it consisted of about a dozen log huts. The town had been laid out some years before but had made no progress. Four-fifths of these low, rude huts were covered with dirt roofs. But one shingle roof was to be found in the place. There were two business houses—general stores—each in their one-room log cabin. So poor had appeared the prospect that even the saloons had passed the place by, only one, quartered in a squalid log house, being found there. McCoy bought the entire town-site for the sum of five dollars an acre. He erected a hotel which he named "Drovers Cottage." There was no one in Abilene capable of managing this tavern; so he sent to St. Louis for one Gore, and his wife Lou. These two became famed among the cattlemen.

By 1867, Abilene was a growing frontier town, wicked and restless. Buildings sprang up, stores were stocked with merchandise, saloons were promptly and plentifully installed. The bad men of the border flocked to the new town. T. C. Henry was elected mayor. He appointed Tom Smith marshal. Smith was fearless, and he established a degree of law and order. But, unfortunately, he was murdered at a critical time in the campaign for law enforcement, and the town relapsed.

In 1871 the people elected McCoy for mayor. He knew of Wild Bill's effective campaign in Hays and it occurred to him that here was the right man for marshal of Abilene. Hickok had often stopped there, and it is likely that he and

McCoy had met more than once. McCoy wanted Hickok
for marshal of Abilene, the city council confirmed the
appointment, and came to an agreement by which Hickok
was to have one hundred and fifty dollars a month, and half
the fines collected in Police Court. Under these conditions
Wild Bill became the marshal, April 15, 1871.

The record of his administration was but poorly kept. The
newspaper of the town was hostile to the Texas cattle business and gave it scant mention. A search of the files fails to
reveal any extended account of the cattle shipments or of the
administration of the town's affairs. This failure of record
makes it difficult properly to treat the administration of
Wild Bill as marshal of Abilene. McCoy in later years said
that Wild Bill had killed forty-three men up to the time of
his appointment. These had been killed in the line of duty as
a peace-officer, and did not include those he had slain in his
service in the Civil War nor Indians killed in scouting on the
Plains. He also asserted that Wild Bill's administration was
satisfactory to him and continued: "Talk about a rule of
iron. We had it in Abilene. We had to rule that way. There
was no fooling with courts of law. When we decided that such
a thing was to be done we did it. Wild Bill cleaned up the
town and kept it clean, but we had to kill a few roughs to do
it." How many men may be included in the term, "a few
roughs," we have now no means of knowing. Abilene admits
but two; but there were undoubtedly more.

There are here and there in the record some glimpses of
Wild Bill in the performance of his duties at Abilene. There
was always a heavy bowie knife with a razor edge concealed
in his sash. He was armed with a sawed-off shotgun and in
addition he sometimes carried a repeating rifle. He patrolled
the streets walking in the center. He knew that he was liable
to be assassinated at any minute. When he entered a building
he always kicked the door back against the wall so that no

one could be concealed there. Once inside, he stood where he could face the entire crowd. He talked little. But what he did say was to the point. The people—the good man and the bad man—quickly learned that he stood solely for order. The business man felt secure with him on guard. The bad man knew that a single break meant death. It was a situation which never before existed in any town in America. It was the iron will of one man holding at bay the malice, crime, and recklessness of the wickedest town on the frontier. A man who passed through this period says, "We were used to seeing men killed because someone disliked their looks, the color of their eyes, cut of their clothes, or the refusal to take a drink, or because they danced too much with one girl." After the arrival of Wild Bill those killings became a thing of the past.

About the first service required of Wild Bill as marshal was to maintain a quorum of the city council. Business was booming and the councilmen could scarcely find time to attend their meetings. One of the councilmen was particularly remiss in this duty. At an important meeting the council was one member short of a quorum. Wild Bill was ordered to produce a quorum. The first councilman he found was this tardy member. He demurred, but Bill marched him to the meeting at the point of his revolver. There, unobserved, the reluctant member slipped away. Bill was immediately directed to produce a quorum. A second time he sought the elusive councilman, who protested volubly. Bill picked him up, threw him across one shoulder and carried him again to the council chamber. There, he sat during the ensuing meeting, pistol in hand. The too-busy councilman also remained.

Susanna Moore rejoined Bill during his stay in Abilene, and together they occupied a little cottage. Also it was in Abilene that Bill met Mrs. Lake. Perhaps it is as well here as at any other place to come to the facts in that matter. Bill

protected her show from the rough element. Mrs. Lake became infatuated with Bill. The friend who went with him to
the Dam said, "Bill was a handsome man, as you know. She
fell for him hard, fell all the way clear to the basement, tried
her best to get him to marry her and run the circus." When
asked why he did not do it, Bill replied, "I know she has a
good show, but when she is done in the West she will go East,
and it is the West for me. I would be lost in the States. No, it
won't do." This friend went on: "I know she was keen for it.
She wrote to him after leaving Abilene. I know, for the letters came in my care under seal to the cottage." So insistent
did she become that Bill induced his friend to tell her that
he was already married—had a wife in Illinois. In this way
only was he able to avoid marrying her without giving of-
fense. If those who had every facility to know can be believed, Mrs. Lake constantly pursued him, and finally
married him.

Here is an incident of Wild Bill's discharge of duty at
Abilene. One night he roughly handled some troublesome
cowboys. They decided to ride into Abilene and hang Bill.
Next morning a number of cowboys met and started to
town. Some say that there were a hundred cowboys in the
mob. There was no real leader, and no plan of action. It
was their belief that Bill would be found in a saloon. They
would seize him and hang him to a telegraph pole. To them
it was a perfectly feasible plan. But Wild Bill knew what was
going on. He went out to the Last Chance Saloon, for there
was the road by which the cowboys would pass. As they approached, Bill stepped out of the saloon with his Winchester
leveled, and a brace of six-shooters in his belt. It was a
cruelly unexpected appearance. Bill called, "Hide out, you
sons of guns!"

The leader, in telling of the event later said, "Every fellow
in our crowd thought Bill meant him, and they all proceeded

to 'hide out.' There was confusion for a minute; the leaders
wheeled their horses; and in the mix-up, each tried to get
the lead going the other way. To them it seemed a long time
before they got strung out. There was no thought of resistance to Bill's order, and soon every member of the band
was hitting the trail for his own camp as fast as his horse
could carry him. So ended the attempt to hang Wild Bill."

It is the proud boast of Abilene that in the days of its
Texas cattle-trade it was the wickedest city in the world.
This may or may not be true, but it was wicked enough.
Certainly there was never another town in Kansas to com-
pare with—not even Dodge City, in its cowboy glory. Its
saloons grew gorgeous with mirrors and cut glass. Mahogany
bars became common. The town acquired sophistication. Its
crudities were interspersed with tawdry and expensive
trappings. The latest devices for lighting were imported and
installed, and great reflectors behind the oil lamps threw
light far into the streets. Expensive gambling paraphernalia
filled the gaming-rooms. Nothing was spared which would
produce a dazzling appearance. The dance-houses never
closed and their scarlet women gave color to the streets.

Some of its saloons were so famous (or infamous) that
memory of them still lives. There was the Alamo where the
Italian and his wife made music on a piano and violin. The
very name was a lure to the cowboy from Texas. The Bull's
Head was owned and operated by Ben Thompson, a Texan
with a long list of murders to his credit, and Phil Coe, a professional gambler of huge proportions and magnificent appearance. It was splendidly equipped, and its faro bank was
said to be the best that money could buy. Within the space of
two blocks about these were thirty others, many of them as
extravagantly furnished. All of the better places had pianos.
Some of them boasted horns; and bull-fiddles roared and
thundered in the chorus. There was the Novelty Theatre. Its

bills were long and gripping. "Six Buckets of Blood, or Who Stabbed the Captain" is said to have been the title of a play presented there and shown in other cattle towns.

It is estimated that in the summer of 1871 there were more than five thousand cowboys in and around Abilene. The streets of the town were congested day and night. People were there from every quarter. Five thousand visitors were in town at one time, and twenty-five hundred were counted in the saloons of one block in an afternoon. And it was this seething horde that Wild Bill and his one deputy held in subjection to order!

The century-old conflict of the man with the hoe against the stockman had been fought out at Abilene by the end of the season of 1871. The man with the hoe had won. The town held an agricultural fair as a demonstration of faith in the possibilities of the soil. In February a published notice was spread broadcast in which the future drovers were practically forbidden to bring cattle to Abilene.

WE, the undersigned, members of the Farmers' Protective Association, and officers and citizens of Dickinson County, Kansas, most respectfully request all who had contemplated driving Texas cattle to Abilene the coming season, to seek some other point for shipment, as the inhabitants of Dickinson County will no longer submit to the evils of the trade.

Texas cattle had made Abilene, had lifted it from a bunch of squalid huts to a thriving city. It was an ungracious dismissal.

But the drovers accepted this deposal with good grace. The end of the sale season had always been celebrated with a round-up—a general gathering in the town to show good will, have a good time, and say good-bye. The round-up this year was to be the greatest of all these post-season gatherings. Wild Bill made the rules and as they were fair and reasonable they were accepted without question. The principal restriction was that there was to be no shooting. There was to be no reckless riding in the streets.

The deposition of the drovers carried with it as a matter of course the exit of the Texas-owned saloons and kindred institutions. The Bull's Head had a standing feud with Wild Bill. He had stood by, pistol in hand, and compelled the repainting of an obscene sign displayed by the management and had at the instance of the City Council forced Coe to bring the faro bank from a back room to the front in the bar-room. And there were other matters of friction, one of which was that with the square deal, the cowboys had broken the faro bank after it had been brought into the light of day. Bill had ruled with an iron hand and lawless institutions are always in secret rebellion against repression of their prac-tices. It was said that an inner circle of Texans, engaged in the saloon business and gambling hells, had conspired to kill Bill on the night of the round-up, and that in selecting the man to carry out the decree the lot had fallen on Coe. Whether this was true or false, or whether the tragedy of the night grew out of the temper of the occasion, will never be known. But bad feeling existed. Coe was the aggressor and brought on the train of events which cost him his life.[1]

It devolved on Pat McGonigal and his brother to give the word to go. They rode up to the Drover's Cottage at sunset, tied their bronchos to the hitching rack, then walked leisurely down Texas Street and met their friends. Their appearance was the signal, and the round-up was on. Jake Karatosky was a Jew and a principal merchant of the town. He was seized and carried to the Applejack saloon and made to treat the crowd. Other citizens shared the same fate. It was all in fun of a rough kind, and no one resented it. All seemed to enjoy this strenuous frolic and roistering merry-making. The bars were crowded and excitement increased.

The revellers sought Wild Bill. It was the intention to carry him to a bar and have a drink with him. He was found at supper in a popular restaurant, but refused in any way to take part in the night's capers, knowing that fun might suddenly change and end in disaster. But he invited them to drink at his expense at the bar of the Novelty Theater and admonished them that shooting was in violation of their pledged word and the city ordinance. The danger-point was reached about ten o'clock. A great mob surged through the town. Texas Street was crowded. The tide was rising and Wild Bill feared it might break beyond control. People sought cover and put out lights. Wild Bill and his deputy, Mike Williams, stood at the Novelty, for trouble was likely to break there if anywhere.

Phil Coe left his own saloon and appeared in front of the Alamo, which was packed with excited men. The air was charged with expectancy. Coe did not enter the Alamo, but stopped in the street and fired his pistol, claiming to have shot at a dog, which was clearly an excuse, for in that crowd there was little room for a dog. Any shot at a dog would have killed or wounded some man. Hearing this shot, Wild Bill ordered Williams to remain on guard at the Novelty, and ran swiftly across to the rear door of the Alamo, which he entered. He demanded the particulars of the shooting, denouncing the bad faith of the cowboys and saloon men.

There was a well just outside the Alamo, and Coe was standing at the curb. When Bill inquired the second time Coe said he had fired the shot; then he fired another, and the ball grazed Bill's side. Bill's action was so swift that his motions could not be followed by the eye. In a flash a pistol was in each hand. The two fired simultaneously—there was but one report. Two balls struck Coe in the abdomen, and Bill exclaimed "I've shot too low." He was at the door when he said this. Instantly he fired two shots at another man just emerging from the darkness and coming swiftly up with two pistols in hand. Coe fired another shot at Bill and missed, then fell across the well-curb. A hundred pistols were drawn and cocked as Wild Bill fired his first shot. By the time he fired the second time the room was cleared and Coe's friends were gone.

The second man shot dropped his pistols, threw both hands above his head, and fell forward dead. It was then that Bill recognized in the stranger, Williams—his deputy whom he had left at the Novelty with orders to remain there. He cried out that he had shot his best friend. He lifted Williams from the floor and laid him on a poker table. He was horror-stricken and grief-stricken.

Now Wild Bill's wrath broke against the Texans. He stalked forth and declared an end to the festivities. He ordered the cowboys from the streets. He was the sword of vengeance—"the blue-eyed Son of the Border had gone wild again." "That night," said Colonel Little, "the desperate heroes of border strife hid in cellars and sunflower patches, or on swift ponies found their way to their cattle camps."

Wild Bill's friends liked to remember him as they saw him that night. Alone, he cleared the town. Plunging into crowds of angry and excited men who he knew wished to take his life, he dispersed and forced them to leave town. He ignored the peril in which he walked. As he strode from street to street—from gambling-house to saloon—lights went out and the town sank to silence.

The town reduced to repose, Bill asked for Coe. Two men had supported him to his rooms. There his clothing was torn apart to find his wounds. When told that there were two bullets in his body he exclaimed: "My father received similar wounds and lived. And I will live." But he was mortally hurt. Hickok sought a clergyman and led him to Coe's bedside. Coe never weakened. He knew soon that he could not recover, but this did not daunt him. He died as other Texans had died, without fear. And among those who felt regret for his death was Wild Bill.

CHAPTER XXIV · *Wild Bill's Show Life*

IN NO part of his life does
Wild Bill's many-sided per-
sonality show more clearly than in his brief career as a showman. His dignity, which decried the profession of an actor;
his sense of humor which continually led him into trouble;
his modesty, which rendered life intolerable for him while
ranting and posing and finally, his love for the plains, which
called to him by day and by night—all these traits are evi-
dent. It is true that at one time Wild Bill had conceived the
idea of owning a show of his own. But how far his idea was
from the real thing is proved by the short record of his attempted ownership of a Wild West exhibition. However,
F. J. Wills gives that abortive project the credit for inspiring
Buffalo Bill's Wild West Show.

In the spring of 1870, tired of Hays City and its hectic
life and having had a winter of leisure and enjoyment at
Topeka, Wild Bill went north from Hays, striking the
Republican River in Nebraska. At Culbertson he secured
men and horses necessary to his scheme and came south to
Beaver Creek. There they found a large herd of buffaloes,
some of which Wild Bill had decided to capture alive. This
he found a much more difficult matter than he had imagined.
Shooting a buffalo would be comparatively simple; taking
the same buffalo alive was an entirely different affair. He
tried to lasso them. This was next to impossible, as they ran
with heads so low that a lariat-loop would not settle over
them. Failure attended most of their efforts. But at last,
after mighty exertion, the party managed to get six angry,

161

frightened buffaloes. Dr. Carver, the Evil Spirit of the Plains, said he was one of the party of Wild Bill's buffalo-catchers. These buffaloes they bound with ropes tied to their horns. After two weeks of strenuous and exciting times, the buffaloes were driven into Ogallala, whence they were shipped *via* the Union Pacific, to Omaha.

Wild Bill had decided on Niagara Falls as the scene of his opening, probably because of the throngs of summer tourists going there. Here, on June twenty-second, he finally landed his buffaloes, along with a few painted and blanketed Comanche Indians. One of these Indians had a trained cinnamon bear, and another a monkey. Wild Bill rented a tract of land on the Canadian shore and built a board corral. Then he advertised a great buffalo chase for July twentieth, and obtained a huge audience. But, unfortunately, he had neglected to build his enclosure high enough to hide his exhibition from the many who came to see and did *not* remain to pay. He was compelled to depend largely on passing the hat for his receipts, an action which showed a misplaced trust in the generosity of man. He came out with a big deficit.

When the performance started the buffaloes, which had been confined in cages, were turned loose. They tore around the inclosure, and the Indians, in gorgeous paint and feathers, pursued on their ponies. So did many of the spectators, most of all the small boys, and all the dogs fortunate enough to be there. It was a large, noisy affair, enjoyed by all present except Wild Bill, and the buffaloes.

In the midst of the excitement, some kind-hearted person, who apparently could not endure seeing a poor animal confined turned loose the bear, which had been muzzled and tied to a post. The bear, overjoyed at his unexpected liberty, started briskly for an Italian who was hawking baked sausages. The Italian, not knowing whether to attribute the bear's attentions to a love of baked sausages or of raw

Italian, threw away his platter and left precipitately. So did most of the other five thousand people present.

Wild Bill found himself broke at the close of the performance. He then and there, as a proprietor, went out of the show business for all time. He sold the buffalo for enough to get the Indians and himself to Kansas City, and went back to the West.

When General Sheridan went from Fort Hays to Chicago, in 1872, he took Buffalo Bill with him as inspector of horses. In Chicago Buffalo Bill met Ned Buntline, whom he had formerly known in the West. Ned Buntline was the author of numerous stories and plays of the dime-novel variety. He was also a lecturer and was at that time giving a series of temperance lectures. The presence of a great scout like Buffalo Bill suggested to him the project of a play which would feature Indians, scouts, plainsmen, and the life of the mighty West. The fruit of this inspiration was a drama entitled, "The Scouts of the Plains."

"The Scouts of the Plains" was written in less than four hours, being intended to make its appeal by the double virtue of the scouts' presence and unstinted action, rather than by elegant diction. Helen Cody Wetmore says that the New York critics were very severe in their reviews. Ned Buntline played the part of "Gale Burg," who was killed in the second act. One paper suggested that it would have been better if this had happened before the play was written. Another offended writer said it was a drama which could begin in the middle and proceed either forward or backward quite as easily and well as the way in which it was written.

But all the criticism must not be heaped on Ned Buntline. A great deal of it was the fault of those untrained and amateur actors, the scouts. They were all the victims of intense stage fright; they forgot their lines, and they made irrelevant remarks and comments—in fact, very little of the original action or dialogue remained after the first production. All in all, perhaps the paper which remarked that the show was so very bad that it was good was justified. But in spite of all this, the show was a huge success. The people liked it— liked the free give-and-take atmosphere, the violent action, the lurid romance, even the ridiculous touches that Wild Bill afterward mischievously added.

Buffalo Bill and Texas Jack (Jack B. Omohundro) had already been touring the states for a season before Wild Bill joined the show. Buffalo Bill makes this statement, but Helen Cody Wetmore says that Wild Bill was with the show in the first season. She writes that Ned Buntline made Buffalo Bill promise the added attraction of Texas Jack and Wild Bill before he would make the contract with the scouts. She says that Wild Bill and Texas Jack were reluctant to join, and that when they finally consented, they preserved the right to leave and go West if the Indians got on the war-path, and they were needed for government service. Ned Buntline not only gave this permission, but offered to join them himself in that event, which pleased them mightily.

The show opened first at Nixon's Auditorium. Then it had its reopening in the fall of 1873 at Niblo's ·Garden. The cast was as follows:

BUFFALO BILL	. W. F. Cody
TEXAS JACK	J. B. Omohundro
WILD BILL	. J. B. HICKOK
PALE DOVE (Wife of Texas Jack)	. Mlle Morlacchi
JIM DAWS, a renegade horse thief	Frank Mordaunt
AUNT ANNIE CARTER	Miss Jennie Fisher
ELLA	Miss Lizzie Safford
LOTTA	Miss Eliza Hudson
UNCLE HENRY CARTER, a friend of the scouts .	. J. V. Arlington
NICK BLUNDER, with song and dance	. Walter Fletcher
TOM DOGGETT, in cahoot with Daws	W. S. McEvoy
EBENEZER LONGLANK, Gov't Peace Commissioner.	. A. Johnson
TALL OAK, a Kiowa, but on the square	. W. A. Reid

BIG THUNDER, a Commanche Chief . . . . B. Meredith
BEAR CLAW, a Commanche Brave . . . . H. Mainhall
RAVEN FEATHER . . . . J. W. Buck

Buffalo Bill was to receive five hundred dollars a week, and
this was increased to a thousand to induce him to accompany
the show to St. Louis. In the second season Ned Buntline
dropped out, and the cast was reorganized.

In an interview with Walter Noble Burns, Buffalo Bill
says that he wrote to Wild Bill at Hays City, on the opening
of the second season, because he had decided that Wild Bill
would make a good actor. "You won't need to do much acting," Buffalo Bill wrote, "you will only have to shoot and
pose around." On receiving Wild Bill's acceptance of the
offer, Buffalo Bill wrote to him again and told him he would
have to quit killing people while he was with the show. Wild
Bill unsmilingly agreed to this; so Buffalo Bill sent him
money and wrote him what to do.

"I am staying at the Brevoort Hotel," he said, "and you
will land in New York at the 42nd St. Depot. To avoid getting lost in the big city, take a cab at the depot and you will
be driven to the hotel in a few minutes. Pay the cabman two
dollars. These New York cabmen are regular hold-up men,
and your driver may want to charge you more, but do not
pay more than two dollars under any circumstances."

Buffalo Bill was glad that his old friend was coming to New
York and entertained the guests at the hotel with stories of
Wild Bill and his feats.

Wild Bill obeyed absolutely the letter of instructions,
which he had committed to memory. When the cab drew up
in front of the hotel, he offered the driver the specified two
dollars.

"Here is your pay," he said.

"Pay nothing," said the cabman, "my charge is five
dollars."

"Well, two dollars is all you're going to get," said Bill.

"Well, Rube, I'll just take the rest out of your hide," said the irate cabman. He climbed down off his box, pulled off his coat and prepared for a fight. He got it. His quiet, grave-faced passenger instantly became a tornado of action. When the dust of the fray had settled, he found himself reposing in the gutter under his horses, from which position he was dragged by jeering spectators.

Wild Bill flicked the dust from his clothes and walked into the lobby of the hotel. The landlord, who had witnessed the little affair, ran hurriedly to Buffalo Bill's room and pounded on the door.

"Say, Mr. Cody," he shouted, "I think the gentleman you've been expecting has arrived."

In this fashion Wild Bill landed in New York to join the show.

Major John Burk, the showman known as "Arizona John," at that time the advance agent for "The Scouts of the Plains," and afterward, for many years, Buffalo Bill's press agent, says of Wild Bill's appearance: "Wild Bill arrived in New York dressed in a cutaway coat, flowered vest, ruffled white shirt, pepper-and-salt trousers, string tie, high-heel boots, and a broad-brimmed hat."

He was thirty-seven years old, at the height of his physical perfection, six feet one inch tall, a magnificent figure of man-hood. He was steel-sinewed, graceful, and light on his feet. His handsome face and long golden-brown locks attracted instant attention. New York literally "sat up and took notice" of him. To the cramped city-dweller he represent-ed the freedom and breadth of the Plains from which he came.

As he was utterly devoid of vanity of desire to become a poseur, his reaction to his unexpected popularity was one of disgusted amazement. To his great discomfiture, crowds followed him in the streets and cheered him on the stage. It was a trial which he bore with marked lack of patience.

"The Scouts of the Plains" followed the accepted lines of marauding Indians, captured travelers, beautiful maidens, and rescuing scouts. It was more or less of a rehash of Robert Montgomery Bird's "Nick of the Woods, or the Jibbenaino-say." There was plenty of red fire and gunpowder and much noise. M. B. Leavitt, who was afterward manager for Buffalo Bill in a subsequent play, "Prairie Waif," and who had opportunities to observe Wild Bill in many performances, writes:

The play that I saw Wild Bill act out was Buffalo Bill's "Scouts of the Plains," written by Ned Buntline. Wild Bill played one of the scouts and had only a few lines. But all the action that he did was very creditable. The play was a sort of Wild West affair, with all the trimmings thrown in; plenty of red fire and Indian fighting. The principals, outside of Cody, were Wild Bill and Texas Jack. Cody was the only real Thespian. The play was well written, a real thriller, and a fine success.

Herbert S. Renton of New Rochelle, New York, states:

As I recall, the formula of the piece was that of Montgomery Bird's "Nick of the Woods; or The Jibbenainosay," which Joe Proctor made so famous, i.e., travelers trapped and abused by Indians, from whose tender mercies they are rescued only in the nick of time. Buntline played a part and I have a vivid remembrance of him tied to a stake, ready for a barbecue, and that he remarked that the Indians were drunk, which furnished a text for a temperance sermon which he delivered then and there. He did not mark the Indians he killed with a cross on the breast as the old jibbanainosay did, but he scored them with his tongue.

Wild Bill was not a good actor. The audience who loved and applauded him were cheering the man himself—not his histrionic ability. Buffalo Bill, in his memoirs, says: "Although he had a fine stage presence, and was a handsome fellow, and possessed a good strong voice, yet it was almost impossible for him to utter a word. He insisted that we were making a set of fools of ourselves, and that we were the laughing-stock of the people."

Wild Bill shunned the spotlight. While he outgrew his first intense stage fright, he was never fully at ease before the footlights. Buffalo Bill was the most adaptable of the three scouts, and in time became a fair actor, though his entrance into stage life was a near failure. J. W. Buel tells the following of the opening night of "The Scouts of the Plains."

"The audience, of course, greeted their appearance with vociferous cheers, and when the noisy ovation subsided, Bill had lost the trail completely and could not remember a single word of his part. But Buntline saw his embarrassment and came to the rescue by speaking foreign to the text.

" 'Where have you been, Bill? What has detained you so long?'

"At this juncture fortune knocked at Bill's door, for seeing Mr. Mulligan, with whom he had hunted only a few weeks before, sitting in a private box, surrounded by several friends he answered:

" 'I've just been out on a hunt with Mr. Mulligan, and we got corralled by a party of hostiles.'

"This answer fairly brought down the house, as Mulligan was one of the best-known business men in Chicago. Both Bill and Buntline saw they had struck a fortunate cue, and that the only way out of their embarrassment was by following this colloquy. Buntline therefore queried:

" 'Is that so? Well, tell us all about the hunt and your escape.'

"Thereupon Bill, who is an excellent story teller and knows just how much ornamentation to give his recitals concerning Indians, related at some length all the particulars that a curious-loving audience could desire, and upon concluding the story there was an encore which shook the house like an explosion."

The stage was set to represent a camp-fire, around which the scouts were grouped. Here they were to tell stories of

Indians and buffalo hunts. To add to the realism, whisky was supposed to circulate freely.

Buffalo Bill tells the following:

We had two or three rehearsals together before Bill made his appearance, and even then he was required to say only a few words. The first scene in which he was cast represented a campfire around which Wild Bill, Texas Jack, and myself were sitting telling stories. In order to carry out the scene so that it should be a faithful counterfeit of the reality, we had a whisky-bottle filled with cold tea which we passed from one to the other at the conclusion of each story. When it came Bill's turn to relate an adventure I passed him the bottle, and taking it in the way with which he was so familiar, he commenced draining the contents. I say commenced, because he stopped very suddenly and spurted the tea right out on the stage, at the same time saying in a voice loud enough for the audience to hear him: "You must think I'm the worst fool east of the Rockies that I can't tell whisky from cold tea. This don't count, and I can't tell a story under the temptation unless I get real whisky." I tried to remonstrate with him, while the audience shook down the galleries with their cheers. At first I was greatly mortified, but it did not take long to convince me that Wild Bill had unconsciously made a big hit. I therefore sent out for some whisky, which Bill drank, and then told his story with excellent effect.

In the play Wild Bill was supposed to rescue a beautiful maiden from the Indians. Every time he fired a shot an Indian fell dead, and when the massacre was complete, Bill was intended to step out to the front of stage, clasp the maiden to his breast, and say:

"Fear not, fair maid. By heavens, you are safe at last with Wild Bill who is ever ready to risk his life, and die, if need be, in defense of weak and helpless womanhood."

This last was a terrible ordeal for Bill, and a mischievous spotlight-man added to his unhappiness by giving him the full benefit of the white glare. For several nights the spotlight man had harrowed Bill's feelings more then usual with his instrument of torture. Finally Bill could stand it no longer. Drawing his pistol, he shot out the spotlight. It was an effective, though startling remedy, and the play proceeded minus the circle of white light.

It was not to be expected that a man of Bill's temperament
and personality would fit very smoothly into the life af the
show. He was too accustomed to dealing punishment to of-
fenders, to tolerate offenses that most people are compelled
to accept. The following instance, which occurred after the
close of the New York season, when the show had taken to
the road, tells how he occasionally broke through the restraint he imposed upon himself. This, also, is one of Buffalo Bill's stories of Wild Bill.

One day at Titusville, Pennsylvania, while Burke, the business agent
was registering our names and making arrangements for our accomoda-
tion, several of us started for the billiard room, but were met by the landlord, who stopped me and said that there was a party of roughs from the
lower oil regions who were spreeing, and had boasted that they were staying in town to meet the Buffalo Bill gang and clean them out. The landlord begged of me not to allow the members of the troupe to enter the
billiard room as he did not wish any fight in his house. To please the landlord, and at his suggestion, I called the boys up into the parlor and ex-
plained to them the situation. Wild Bill wanted to go at once and fight
the whole mob, but I persuaded him to keep away from them during the
day.

In order to entirely avoid the roughs the members of the company
entered the theater through a private door from the hotel, as the two buildings joined each other. While I was standing at the door of the theater
taking tickets, the landlord came rushing up and said that Wild Bill was
having a fight with the roughs in the bar-room. It seemed that Bill
had not been able to resist the temptation of going to see what kind of a
mob is was that wanted to test the pluck of Buffalo Bill's party; and just
as he stepped into the room, one of the bruisers put his hand on Bill's
shoulder and said: "Hello, Buffalo Bill; we have been looking for you all
day."

"My name is not Buffalo Bill; you are mistaken in the name," was the
reply.

"You're a liar!" said the bruiser.

Bill instantly knocked him down, and then seizing a chair, he laid out
four or five of the crowd on the floor, and then drove the rest out of the
room. All this was done in a minute or two, and by the time I got down-
stairs, Bill was coming out of the bar-room, whistling a lively tune.

"Well!" said he, "I have been interviewing that party that wanted to
clean us out."

"I thought you promised to come into the Opera House by the private entrance?"

"I did try to follow that trail, but I got lost among the canyons, and then I ran in among the hostiles," said he. "But it's all right now; they won't bother us any more."

We heard no more of them after that.

The show toured the principal cities and towns of the East and Middle West, and wherever the performance was given it met with great success. But of the three scouts, only Buffalo Bill was contented and at home on the stage. Wild Bill remained unhappy and homesick for his former life. Daily he grew more moody and dejected. He developed a vast boredom. Life grew steadily more unbearable. His temper became that of a harried wildcat.

The different authorities who have written of Wild Bill make diverse statements regarding the causes for his rupture with the exhibition. But they unite on one point, i.e., his intense and ever-growing distaste for the life of an actor.

Helen Cody Wetmore says that Wild Bill had been pleading with Major John Burk for some time to release him. But that experienced old showman was far too wise deliberately to deprive his performance of a star attraction. Wild Bill at last saw the futility of his request and resolved to make himself so unbearable that, in self-defense, the proprietor would break the contract and discharge him.

Accordingly he resumed his old trick of shooting the supers at close range, and added to this many other ingenious variations on the routine performance. The rest of the cast began to dread each show time, wondering what new and startling turn Wild Bill might introduce into the already too vivid action. In fact, Wild Bill employed all the tactics of a mischievous small boy who desires his liberty.

Remonstrance did no good. Bill stated mildly that "he never hurt the fellows any." And if they objected to him, of course *they* were free to leave.

In the spring of 1874 the show was at Rochester, New
York. While there Wild Bill again met Mrs. Lake who, being
in Rochester at that time, went to see the show. According to
J. W. Buel, Buffalo Bill discovered the lady in the audience,
and, knowing Wild Bill's acquaintance with her, immediately
arranged the meeting. Buel says that Wild Bill proposed
marriage to Mrs. Lake, but that, because of her confused
financial affairs which would require at least two years to
straighten, she refused him. From this time on his account
of Wild Bill's last performance practically coincides with that
of Helen Cody Westmore. He writes in full:

When he was called for his part during the same evening's performance, he
resumed his old annoying practice of singeing the "supers" legs, and carried
the trick so far this time that Buffalo Bill remonstrated so sharply, that,
without saying a word, Wild Bill doffed his buckskin suit, and resuming
his usual dress, walked out of the theatre, refusing to appear any more
with the combination. Before he left Rochester, however, Buffalo Bill and
Texas Jack made up a purse between them of one thousand dollars, and
gave it to him as an evidence of their continued friendship.

Mrs. W. F. Cody adds a bit more detail to the above. She
writes that one night he was standing in the wings talking
to her. He had just come off the stage after stammering his
way through his part. He turned a jaundiced eye on Buffalo Bill and Texas Jack, who were still on the stage, and
said grimly:

"Ain't they right foolish? What's the use of getting out
there and making a show of ourselves? I ain't going to do it
any more!"

With which he changed his buckskins for his scarcely less
picturesque attire of every day, and quietly walked away
from the show forever.

Ed Moore was an old soldier and for many years a newspaper man, who lived long in Topeka. He died at the National Military Home, Leavenworth, in 1927. He gave an
altogether different cause for Bill's severing his relations with

the show. And in his statement lay the real reason for Buel's incorrect statement that Wild Bill suffered from ophthalmia.

Moore, in a statement made to the author, said that in 1873 or 1874 (most probably in 1874), one of the lamps of the footlights exploded and nearly burned Bill's eyes out. This was at Rochester, New York. He was in the hospital for some time and was compelled to wear thick-lensed glasses until his eyes began to regain their strength.

It is also from Moore's account that the following incident is taken: Along in August of 1874 (may have been in 1875), Wild Bill, Moore, and some particular cronies were present at the fair grounds, southwest of Kansas City, where they had gone to see the horse races. Bill was just back from Rochester, and his eyes were not yet well. It seems that his right eye was the one more injured. Wild Bill was not the sort of person to take care of glasses, and the lens of the right eye was gone. Bill donned the glasses to watch the races, with the remark that he couldn't see at all without his specs. One of the party then stuck his finger through the empty frame to prove to Bill that the glass was gone. Bill threw the glasses away in disgust, and said,

"Come on, boys, the treat's on me!"

With that, the entire party adjourned to the nearest bar for liquid refreshment.

But one of the main causes of Bill's departure from the show was his never-ceasing longing for the Great Plains. The sense of vast space and freedom; the rhythmical swing of his pony, carrying him tireless miles through the long silences of starlit nights; the tiny smoke-spiral rising from his camp-fire beside some stream fringed with rustling cottonwoods—for Bill, the thought of any one of these carried acute nostalgia. And he yearned for the garish lights and hectic night life of the flimsy cowboy towns, the excitement, and the danger. In plain words he was desperately homesick.

Buel writes that after Bill left Rochester with the thousand dollar purse that had been given him, he once again tried his fortune with a show. However, many authorities dispute this. But the Buel statement is interesting, and says, in detail:

Being considerably flush for a scout, Wild Bill went to New York, and while there, in a very laudable effort to break a faro bank, got himself ingloriously "busted." In this condition a theatrical manager approached him with a liberal proposition, so that for a second time he became a votary of Thespis, coming again before the public with the Wild Bill combination. But he had evidently struck a blind pocket of ill luck, for after a few fitful weeks of uncertainty the concern became pecuniarily defunct. After Bill had left the new combination, the manager immediately reorganized his troupe and replaced Wild Bill by a cheaper character. Everywhere the company performed they advertised the renowned Wild Bill as their leading star, a member of the troupe being engaged to personate the distinguished scout on and off the stage alike. Wild Bill was not long in learning this trick and at once decided to get satisfaction by undeceiving the deceiver. Accordingly, learning that the company was to appear at Binghamton, New York, he went there to witness the performance. Waiting until the plot was developing much interest to the audience, when the bogus Wild Bill was shooting and slashing his way through a band of howling Comanches, he leaped upon the stage and, grabbing the manager, flung him bodily into the orchestra, and then knocked the personator of his character through the scenes, regardless of the knives and pistols and tomahawks carried by the Indians.

This novel procedure precipitated an intermission, during which Bill unconcernedly resumed his seat and shouted to the company to proceed with the show.

Information of the interruption having reached the municipal officers, a policeman was sent up to arrest Bill. He was easily found, but when the officer asked him to consider himself under arrest the reckless scout replied:

"How numerous are you?"

"I am alone; why do you ask?"

"Well, I would advise you to call up some assistance."

The policeman took his advice and went out and soon returned with a brother officer. The two then approached Bill and asked him to accompany them.

"How numerous are you now?" Bill asked.

"There are two of us."

"Then I would advise you to go out on another recruiting expedition."

The two policemen, anxious to avoid a conflict with the noted scout,

then called the sheriff, who requested Bill to submit to arrest, and had no
difficulty in taking him out of the theater and keeping him in charge until
the following morning, when his trial took place before the city judge. The
circumstances of the row having been detailed, Bill was fined three dollars
and costs, but his satisfaction in punishing the bogus character more than
compensated him for his expense and trouble.

F. J. Wilstach gives an account of the following incident,
but states that it was never proved. However, it is a very
generally accepted anecdote. His version practically agrees
with that of Buel, given below.

Leaving the East, Bill went directly to Kansas City, and from there to
Cheyenne, a place he had not visited for several years. Here he drifted to
a faro bank which was run by a gambler named Bowlby. Bill had only two
hundred dollars with him, and he commenced the game by staking small
amounts. Losing all these, he played up for an average by doubling.
Staking fifty dollars he also lost that, but immediately put down another
fifty-dollar bill. Bowlby, who was banking, told Bill, who was a stranger
to him, that the limit was twenty-five dollars, and that he could not play
above that sum.

"Why," inquired Bill, "didn't you just take fifty dollars of my money?"

"Well," said Bowlby, "I won't let you play that amount any more."

"You won't?" replied Bill, "then I'll see why; that fifty dollar bill lays on
the tray and if my card don't turn, the money is yours but if it does come
out, then I'll have fifty dollars of your money or there'll be fun here, that's
all."

From this a war of words followed, until Bill struck Bowlby on the
head with a heavy walking cane, which rolled him off a substantial seat.
Several bouncers for the establishment rushed upon Bill, but he knocked
them in a most artistic manner, until finding the fighting too progressive
he jumped into a corner and jerked out two pistols. At this juncture the
barkeeper, attending the saloon downstairs, hearing the noise, ran up and
discovering the situation, cried out:

"Look out, boys, that's Wild Bill!"

This information acted like magic; the tempest was becalmed and a
moment later Bill was alone.

On the following day, Bowlby, although still nursing a badly damaged
head, called on Bill and producing champagne and cigars, the two settled
their difference amicably.

Another account of the same incident states that in the
furore Wild Bill's hat was knocked off, his mane of tawny hair

tumbled over his shoulders, and the crowd recognized him. The hostilities ceased with startling abruptness, and the fighters faded away with the swiftness displayed by men, who, teasing a supposed dog, discover their prey to be a lion. There was no ostentation about their passing. One minute they occupied the same room with Wild Bill, the next minute Wild Bill occupied the room alone.

This same account states that instead of trying to placate Wild Bill, the outraged Bowlby sought the aid of the town marshal, stating that in the mêlée Wild Bill had scooped up all the money on the faro table, some seven hundred dollars, and had carelessly neglected to return it afterwards. Together, they sought Wild Bill, who received them calmly, and without urging, acknowledged the truth of the accusation.

"You ought not to come ambuscadin' into camp that a-way," he said. "Your bashful entrance into town might have got a passel of Cheyenne people killed. It wasn't right, Mr. Hickok. Only it's you, I'd say it sort of bordered on the treacherous."

Then Mr. Bowlby timidly spoke up.

"It ain't that I'm askin' it back, Mr. Hickok, but I want to check up my game," he said. "sech bein' my motive, would you-all mind informin' me kindly how big a wad you got outen that drawer?"

"Which I sure can't say," replied Bill. "I haven't counted it as yet." Then in a friendly way he said, "Mr. Bowlby, I don't reckon that I ought to keep all that money; it's too much. I'd feel easier if you would let me split it with you."

"No objections in the least," replied Mr. Bowlby, politely.

"Which I should say as much!" exclaimed the marshal in enthusiastic admiration of Bill's liberality. "Thar's an offer that is good enough for a dog. An' now, gents," concluded the marshal, linking one arm into that of Bill and hooking Mr.

Bowlby with the other, "let's go down to the Gold Room an' licker."

In the portion of this narrative devoted to Abilene, and Wild Bill's life there, the incident of Phil Coe is detailed at length. At that time a party of the friends of Phil Coe vowed vengeance on Wild Bill. As he left shortly after that for the East, there was no time to settle the affair, and the friends of Coe spread to the winds the rumor that Wild Bill had gone because he feared them.

While Wild Bill was in the East, he was apprised by one of his friends that these Texans had vowed to meet him immediately on his return—if he ever did return—and settle the difference. This was so agreeable a solution of the matter to Wild Bill that he wrote them, telling them when he would arrive at Cheyenne.

Accordingly, when the train pulled into Cheyenne, Wild Bill stepped to the rear platform, ready to accomodate the friends of Coe. But being cautious men and wise, they were as far from Cheyenne that day as surrounding space would permit. A large crowd of noncombatants who had gathered to witness the fray applauded and so Wild Bill's entry into Cheyenne was in the nature of an ovation.

In this manner ended Wild Bill's life as a showman. It was a broadening experience, of course. Wild Bill had added a new chapter to his book of knowledge. And he had lost none of his sense of justice, nor his lightning-swift impulse to punish the offender against it. He was still the ruthless dealer of merited punishment to "bad men" both white and red. The show life of the East gave him back to the West, more sophisticated, quieter, graver, with a greater scope of vision.

He had always known he would return. Released, he had winged his flight to the Great Plains as surely as the eagle to his nest. There he took up his life where he had dropped it to make this fantastic excursion into the realms of make-believe.

CHAPTER XXV · *Wild Bill at Ellsworth,*
Dodge City, Wichita—
Miscellaneous

WILD BILL spent a part
of the winter of 1871–
72 in Kansas City. He was often in Topeka and Leavenworth.

In 1872 Colonel Lindsay was stationed for a time at Ellsworth. This town had fallen heir to the cattle-shipping business discarded by Abilene, though Ellsworth never equaled Abilene in fame as a cattle town. Ben Thompson, the outlaw partner of Phil Coe in the saloon and gambling business in Abilene, had a brother, Gill Thompson, who was proprietor of a disreputable place in Ellsworth in 1872 and later. Thompson was a noisy, self-assertive man. When in liquor he was a dangerous man. At Ellsworth he was known as "Bully" Thompson.

One day at Ellsworth Colonel Lindsay went into a saloon to get a drink of whisky. At a table sat a desperado known as Bob Dunlap. A few minutes after Colonel Lindsay entered this resort Wild Bill came in. He was surprised to see the Colonel there.

He seemed to know that trouble was expected and said it might be serious. About that time a ruffian bolted in and began to talk vulgarly and insultingly to the crowd. He announced that he was "Bully" Thompson and ended by saying, "Come up and have a drink with the toughest man on the Plains." Everyone except Dunlap went up to the bar. Seeing that "Bob" apparently had no intention of coming forward, Thompson roared,

178

[SUTLER'S STORE AT DODGE CITY, FROM AN OLD PRINT]

"Did you hear my invitation to all the sons of sea-cooks in here to come up and drink!"

"Yes," said Bob, "but if I want to drink I can buy it myself. I don't have to drink unless I want to, do I?" With that they began to fight. Bill and Lindsay were standing with their backs against the bar, a little apart. The fight was a terrible one. Both men were left bruised and bleeding. Bob finally conquered.

Wild Bill said to Lindsay, "Let's go. I thought there might be a rough-house but this was a poor affair. I could have whipped them both in just one minute. This is getting to be a tame town."

Colonel Lindsay also gave this incident to the author. He had a fine spirited young horse named Jerry, which Wild Bill rode one day when he went with a party to hunt buffaloes. Instead of buffaloes a large herd of elk was found. The hunters charged the herd, and Wild Bill shot a large bull elk which went down, apparently dead. Bill rode up and dismounted to cut the elk's throat. Jerry's bridle rein fell over one of the elk's hind feet. When Wild Bill touched the elk it sprang up and started to run. Jerry's bridle rein was still around its hind leg. Bill did not know at first why the horse was following the elk and called "Whoa! Jerry." When he saw what the trouble really was he knew he could not kill the elk, for it was running directly from him. To release the horse he shot the bridle rein in two. He then mounted Jerry, pursued the elk, and gave it a fatal shot. This incident has been preserved in some of the books on the West and has sometimes been declared an impossibility. When this matter was brought to the attention of Colonel Lindsay he assured the writer that the incident had occured, that the horse was his own and did not belong to Wild Bill.

Colonel Lindsay was often with Wild Bill on buffalo hunts. Bill's method of killing a buffalo was to ride against the animal and shoot it through the heart with a Colt's revolver. He always shot the buffalo just back of the angle made by the junction of the front leg and shoulder—The heart was close there and easily hit. Wild Bill said to Colonel Lindsay, "Cody kills buffalo with a rifle. I can kill six buffalo with a revolver while he is killing one with his rifle."

Ben Thompson, the partner of Phil Coe, was in Ellsworth in 1873 and was in charge of the saloon and gambling house established the previous year with his money by his brother, Bully Thompson. He had committed many murders, and was the most notorious man in the underworld of Ellsworth. His place in Ellsworth had a bad reputation, and it was believed that drovers were often robbed there. He said Wild Bill should never pass through the town. When told of this threat Wild Bill notified Thompson that he would be on a certain train on a certain day.

Ben Thompson boasted that he would go on the train and kill Wild Bill in revenge for the death of Phil Coe. A prominent attorney, still living in the town, was anxious to see how the matter would turn out, and he was at the station when this passenger train pulled into Ellsworth. Ben Thompson and a number of his associates went through the train. They said that they had failed to find Wild Bill. Men on the train reported that they did find Wild Bill but did not disturb him. He was not molested and the ruffians left.

Here is another story told the writer by the gentleman from Ellsworth. Wild Bill was in Junction City frequently and for weeks at a time. A stalwart and muscular civilian involved Bill in a dispute over some unimportant matter. He told Bill that if he would take off his guns he would give him a thrashing. Bill quietly removed his revolvers, handed them to a bystander, and the two began to fight with their fists. Bill had an easy time of it. He knocked the man down and disposed of him with little effort.

The Reverend John A. Anderson was a Presbyterian minister in Junction City. Afterwards he was in charge of the State Agricultural College, was elected to Congress, and was Consul to Cairo, Egypt. In the days of his ministry he wished to raise a considerable sum of money for his church. He enlisted the services of Wild Bill, who collected quite a large sum of money and turned it over to Anderson, who was always afterward the friend and champion of Wild Bill.

After Wild Bill quit the show business he was much in Colorado and Wyoming. He became well known in Denver but held no office there. He was in other towns of Colorado and was sometimes in Cheyenne. Investigation of his life has failed to disclose any trouble for him or with him at either place, except when he threw the card game into a panic, picked up all the winnings, and walked off.

John Wesley Hardin was a Texas "bad man." He left an account of his life. In his book there is given an incident of Abilene. Hardin says it was in the spring of 1871, and that he went in with a Texas herd of longhorns. Hardin became drunk and noisy soon after reaching Abilene. Here is what he says happened to him:

Wild Bill tapped him on the shoulder and quietly told him he was under arrest, and to take off his guns. Hardin complied, but—handing the pistols to Bill butt foremost, when Bill reached for them Hardin reversed them suddenly by a trick known as the "road-agent spin." Hardin had his pistols in his hands and pointed at Bill—had the drop on him. Then he reviled Bill—called him a long-haired coward, said he would shoot a boy in the back. Bill was at his mercy . A crowd of desperate men assembled shouting and demanding that Hardin kill Wild Bill. Bill implored Hardin to save him. Hardin called out that he would kill anyone who interfered. They went into the saloon where Bill assured Hardin he

would not be arrested for any Texas crime and that he
might wear his guns.

All of which is only the boast and brag of Hardin. The
arrest occurred in the usual way and Hardin submitted as
tamely as a rabbit. It is safe to say that if Hardin could
have killed Bill with safety to himself he would have done so.
Nothing else would have given him such fame—especially in
Texas, where he wanted it. Then, the "road-agent spin" was
old stuff in Wild Bill's day. Every peace-officer knew it and
guarded against it. Wild Bill was never caught by any such
cheap trick.

Wild Bill was never a resident of Dodge City. As a scout
he often passed over the site upon which Dodge City was
established, but in those days there was no Dodge City. He
drove freight-trains and passenger stages over the site in his
services over the old Santa Fé Trail, but the town had not
then come out of chaos. Bill, in his Indian scouting,
was often at Fort Dodge, six miles from where Dodge City
was later laid out. But with Dodge City, Wild Bill never was
associated. He visited his old-time friend, Bob Wright,
there once, and remained a few days. He played poker with
Wright and, together they visited some gambling-rooms
around town. But he never had any adventure nor trouble
at Dodge City. His visit to Wright was in 1874 or 1875 for
only a few days.

A frontier character named "Garibaldi" Smith was a warm
friend of Wild Bill. He had been associated with Bill as scout
on the Plains. He went to live at Dodge City when that town
was established. He said that Wild Bill paid him a visit there
and remained some time as his guest.

The only event at Dodge City which was in any way connected with Wild Bill occurred while he was on this visit to
"Garibaldi" Smith. This story is of doubtful authenticity,
and it may never have happened. But it persists, and so it is

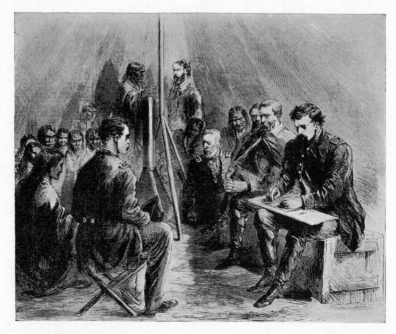

[INDIAN COUNCIL AT FORT DODGE, FROM AN OLD PRINT]

given here. One evening Bill called on a druggist who happened to be mayor of the town. The mayor had taken some action which angered the gamblers and saloon keepers. They sent notice that they would call that particular evening. This notice bore a threatening air. Wild Bill called at the drug store to visit his friend, arriving a few minutes before the delegation appeared. He and the mayor were in a back room in quiet conversation when the crowd came in. The mayor went out to meet his hopeful fellow-townsmen, who addressed him harshly and with rising wrath. Hearing which, Wild Bill sauntered forth with a smile and said casually to the leader: "Hello, Jake! Ain't it a little crowded in here!" Bill had no visible weapon except his smile. But those nearest the door went noiselessly out. Others followed. In less than a minute after Wild Bill entered, the store was cleared, and he and the mayor resumed their conversation in the back room.

So, the Dodge City life of Wild Bill must be relegated to the long list of events in his life which never happened.

Precisely the same must be said of his life at Wichita.

CHAPTER XXVI · *Calamity Jane*

THE tendency of the modern romancer when he deals with the people who, a few short years ago, lived and acted out their diverse parts on the stage of the Great Plains, is to drape a veil of illusion over all. Then, out from under this rosy veiling step gunman, gambler, cowboy, soldier, Indian, dance-hall girl—all who were part of the great panorama of the frontier. But how changed! The men, whether cast as heroes or villains, all handsome, or at least picturesque, the women, unfailingly young, charming, and of dazzling beauty.

All this is not only absurd, but unnecessary. None of the characters need don this make-up to live most vividly again in book or play. The Plain man or woman, as he or she existed at that period, often rough, weather-beaten, uncouth, is a figure of far greater romance than any writer of fiction has ever created.

So we can discard that coy charmer, the buckskin clad belle of the Plains whom so many writers have fused into Calamity Jane, and yet have a fascinating woman, and a most interesting personality, with whom to deal.

Calamity Jane was the product of frontier life. Her life mirrored her environment. Although in any setting she would have stood out as an unique person, the Old West was peculiarly suited to her development. To-day she typifies the Old West as truly as does the memory of the cowboy, the dance-hall girl, the two-gun man, or Indian. Her name is as suggestive of romance to the imaginative as the sight of a heap of bleaching buffalo bones, a time-decayed covered wagon by the side of the trail, a lone Indian pony posed against a sunset sky.

Her great tragedy is that she outlived her time. It is most unmerciful to judge her by the standard that the New West established during the last twenty years of her life. It is cruel to exploit her as some of the younger writers have recently done. She lived out her last days, when she had grown too old to change, in a new and complicated world. Gone was the Indian, the buffalo, the scout; gone the free life of camp and fort and cowboy-town; gone the click of the roulette wheel and clink of glasses on the bar. The saloon, the gambling-house, the dance-hall with its blaring music, and the companionship these had held for her with her own kind—they had disappeared as completely as though such a life had never been. Had she spent her latter days on a desert island, she could not have been more lonely nor forlorn.

Calamity Jane was born at Princeton, Missouri, about 1850. She was christened Martha Canary, and was the eldest of a family of six children. When she was thirteen years old, her parents became victims of the Montana gold fever; so they disposed of their possessions, and started, the whole family, in a covered wagon. It was a long, hard trip, and it was during that time that Martha first learned to ride and shoot and watch for hostile Indians. Throughout the slow, inefficient progress, it was she who supplied their larder with game. It was her first taste of her future and in spite of hardship, and overwork, and danger, she liked it.

They had scarcely reached Montana, however, when the mother of the family died. The father, left struggling alone, grew daily poorer and less able to cope with the situation. Fortune frowned upon him, and in the futile, dazed gestures he made against her, he lost nearly all their few belongings. At last, in despair, he gathered his children together and started back home to Old Missouri.

The pitiful little procession was stopped at Salt Lake City by the death of Martha's father. And by his loss the burden of the young family was shifted to Martha's shoulders. While but a child herself, she was confronted with the problem of feeding and clothing five younger children.[1] Martha seized the first honest work at hand, which happened to be dish-washing in the grub houses at Fort Bridger. She buckled to this none-too-dainty task with grim determination, and the children were given a home of sorts, and enough food to live. When this work became too hideous to endure longer, she hired out as cook at different ranches; she washed, she scrubbed, in fact, she did any and everything that would help to drive away the wolf of want from the door of her younger sisters and brothers. Some accounts say that the soldiers helped her out a bit with her slender means.

But through all this, she was learning steadily. Learning to ride like an Indian, to shoot quick and straight, to be ever alert, to stand hardship and danger and exposure. She obtained a great stock of Indian lore: she became expert at tracking her prey, at hunting, at woodcraft, and in camp life. The cowboys, the soldiers, the gamblers, the bartenders and gunmen were her teachers. Many of her lessons were learned at the bar of some saloon. She had no women friends. She would have been as awkward and ill-at-ease in her relations with the conventional "ladylike" woman of that period as would some gawky country boy. Her future creed of life was got from experience—hard, bitter, aging experience.

And to the vast mass of knowledge she gained, she added several accomplishments. She took the greatest pride in her ability to out-chew, out-smoke, out-swear and out-drink most of her masculine companions. Her profanity, in particular, was so rich in metaphor, and so varied, that it was a source of artistic delight to discriminating audiences. If she happened to lack for the right word, which happily seldom

happened, it was hastily supplied by some awed admirer of
the eruption, and the air continued to crackle and turn blue.
Even at this time she was gifted to a remarkable degree with
the talent of carrying her liquor well. Many times when she
drank with her peers, they were left "down among the dead
men" under the table or bar, while Martha triumphantly
erect staggered home.

In 1870, Martha's family was independent enough that
she was at liberty to follow her own inclinations. This led
her to discard the dress of a woman for the more grateful
buckskins, chaps, and spurs of her associates. And she very
seldom at any time of her life thereafter re-donned feminine
trappings.

Indoor life was abhorrent to her; and so she went to several
forts, seeking the employment for which she was best fitted—
that of a government scout. Though her ability and skill
were undoubtedly far greater than that of many of her associates, the fact that she was a woman kept her from getting
on the staff of any general until she arrived at Fort D. A.
Russell, Wyoming. Here she was hired and had performed
some splendid work before her sex became known. Then, as
she had made herself an invaluable aid to the soldiers, she
was still retained. It is doubtful if Custer ever had a better
scout.

She asked no privileges, no favors. Modesty, as the term
is generally used, simply did not exist for her, and she was
perfectly at home, rolled in a blanket asleep by a camp-fire,
in the company of a troop of soldiers. Her accomplishments
of profanity, and straight shooting first, with explanations
later, were ample protection for her.

Not that she often needed them. The men accepted her
as one of themselves. She was a warm friend, ready to grub-
stake the pal who was "broke," to care for and nurse any
down-and-out who needed it. She was equally quick to

mother some homesick boy or punish the one who would tor-
ment him. And the men felt no need of restraint in conversation carried on before her. She spent her money freely in
gambling and drinking, it is true, but there was always
enough left to give some poor chap a lift.

Martha was the first white woman to enter the Black
Hills. She went as a scout for the United States Army on the
campaign of 1872. And it was here, and in the following
fashion, that she got the name of "Calamity Jane." One day,
a group of scouts, including Martha, were in advance of the
soldiers near Goose Creek, in Wyoming. They had entered
a deep wooded canyon, where they were suddenly surrounded
by Indians. In the ensuing fight and flight, Captain Charles
Egan, in command, was wounded, and fell from his horse.
Two Indians immediately swooped down to scalp him.
Martha saw what had happened, wheeled, dropped on her
pony's neck, Indian fashion, and dashed back into the Indian
fire. She shot one Indian, and stooping, dragged Captain
Egan up from the ground, across her saddle. She rode back
fearless and erect, defiant of the Indian bullets, and rejoined
her companions.

When Captain Egan was well enough to understand, he
was told that he had been rescued by a woman. He called her
to him, and said. "Well, Jane, you are a good one to have
around in time of calamity." The soldiers promptly dubbed
her Calamity Jane, and she was intensely proud of the name.

Calamity Jane was a vigorous, strong woman, and was
never sick but once. Strangely enough, that one illness saved
her life. In 1876 she was sent with government dispatches
from General Crook to Generals Custer, Miles, and Terry,
then on the Big Horn. The trip was made in the dead of
winter, and in the intense cold she was compelled to swim the
swollen, icy Platte River. She arrived at her journey's end,
burning and shivering, half delirious, but faithful in the ful-

fillment of her trust. It was pneumonia that developed, and for many days she was dangerously ill. Then there was a long convalescence. It was during this time that Custer and his men were massacred at the Little Big Horn. Had she not been ill, Jane most surely would have been there, too.

The final defeat of the Sioux in 1891 brought her career as a government scout to its close. There was no further need for scouts; and so this greatest of woman scouts found herself at loose ends. Some of her comrades, faced with the same situation, became pony express riders; some took up freighting; others went back to farming or mining.

In 1879, fire swept Deadwood, and a little later, smallpox ravaged it. Calamity Jane laid aside her guns and became a nurse—an awkward one, but endlessly gentle and patient. Out of her own small resources, she took money for food and medicines for those too poor to buy their own. She worked long and bravely, going constantly from one house to another on her errands of kindness. At the end of the siege, she asked for a leave of thirty days in which to revisit her old home in Missouri. It was granted, but the visit was a great disappointment to Jane. Calamity and the women of the little stagnant Missouri town had nothing in common. They regarded her as a curiosity, and were repelled by her uncouth and masculine ways. She, on her part, found no interest in their tame and restricted lives. She viewed with contempt all domesticity. So, long before the end of her vacation, she was back in Deadwood again.

Jane now adopted the pony express as the most exciting existence left in a changing world. For a year she carried the mail between Deadwood, South Dakota, and Custer, Montana. Later, when that employment failed, she found work with a freighting firm operating from Westport Landing out across the Plains. For four years she drove a six-mule team, and her highly finished mode of handling the "black-snake" and reins was much admired by her fellow-teamsters. If it is true that mule-driving requires an immense and profane vocabulary, then surely Jane was fitted for the place.

It was to be expected that a gold-rush would appeal to such a person as Jane. She gave up her work with the freighting firm and went to Central City, Colorado, at the beginning of the "boom." Here she staked out a claim and started to sink a shaft. A cautious and covetous gentleman named Ragan, wanting a claim, and being far too discreet to try to take one from some man, decided that Jane would be easy prey. He promptly "jumped" hers. Had he but known, the "sport" who pulled the wildcat's whiskers under the impression that it was a "nice kitty" probably had a safer bet. It is certain he would have found juggling with chain lightning much less exciting and much more quiet and safe.

A joyous and expectant messenger brought the gratifying news to Calamity Jane, at ease in her favorite saloon. Calamity wasted no time. She reached for her belt, with its arsenal Colt's .44's, strapped it in place, and strode to the shaft. On the brink, she stopped and hailed the gentleman below.

"What are you doing down there, you dirty polecat?" she asked.

"I'm digging for gold. What the hell did you suppose I'm doing?" was the gentle response.

"Will you come up, or do you want to be buried down there?" queried Calamity briskly.

Ragan, annoyed at this persistence, glanced up—into the muzzle of a large business-like gun. He came up. Promptly. Calamity Jane marched him to jail, with the gun jabbing him uncomfortably in the back. Undoubtedly she found deep and soothing joy in his comments. No more "claim jumpers" came to trouble the peaceful operations of Jane's mine.

But, for all its gallant defense, the mine proved a failure. In this it was not alone, for the whole "boom" collapsed.

Jane's "stake" was lost along with her dreams of ease and wealth. For a time she drifted aimlessly from one camp to another. She was drinking more heavily all the time, and not carrying it well.

She had passed the zenith of her life and was on the long down-grade that was to end so pitifully near the bottom. She was at Deadwood for a little time; after that she made a brief stay at Blackfoot, Montana. Then she disappeared from sight for several years. Those casual bits of news concerning old friends and foes exchanged before the bars of various saloons held no mention of Calamity Jane.

It was not until 1895 that she made her final re-entry on our stage at Deadwood. To the stunned amazement of her old associates, she had acquired a husband and a small daughter in the interim. The lucky man was a Clinton Burke, a cab driver, of El Paso, Texas. In spite of the fervid interest manifested by those to whom Calamity in the rôle of house-wife and mother was a complete anachronism, Jane herself maintained a most discreet silence. And because of her chariness in regard to details, the particulars of her romance are shrouded in mystery.

But there was one undisputed fact apparent to all who came in contact with her at this period, and that was her devotion to the little daughter. Calamity lavished on her the motherliness that formerly she had spread to cover all who came to her in need of it. She displayed immense pride in the child.

She finally placed her in a girl's school, at Sturgis, South Dakota. There are many rumors and theories concerning Calamity Jane's daughter and her ultimate fate. Whether she was ashamed of her mother, as she grew older, and so deserted her, or whether Jane recognized herself as a detriment to the girl's advancement and deliberately severed the bond will never be known. It is known, however, that Jane

cared for her and educated her, and always remained loving
and proud of her.

Soon after her return to Deadwood she divorced Burke,
as she was unable to stand the monotony of an unduly pro-
tracted spell of matrimony. There have been many stories
about Calamity Jane's husbands, some people giving her
credit for as many as twelve, all of whom met violent deaths.
But only Burke is really known to have married her, and the
other tales are the product of that type of writer who also
filled the yellow-back of that period with eulogiums of her
grace and beauty.

As to Calamity Jane's relations with Wild Bill, it is absolutely untrue that he ever, at any time, was in love with
her. It is also extremely doubtful that she ever cared for him
in that sense. But it is true that they liked and admired each
other immensely. They were of the same breed—generous,
brave, fiery, quick to avenge an insult or protect a friend.
They shared a common existence. They performed the same
duties, they faced the same dangers. And each had sufficient
knowledge of the hardships of the life of a scout to admire
whole-heartedly the other's courage and skill.

When Wild Bill was shot, at the old Bella Union saloon,
at Deadwood, Calamity Jane was among the first to reach
the spot. While the men hesitated to pursue the assassin,
fearful for their own lives, Jane started into raging, fiery-
hearted action. Her mingled grief and fury left no room in
her heart for fear. In her hurry she had left her weapons behind and was completely unarmed. But that did not deter
her. She went after her man, just the same, defiant and unafraid of his guns, still smoking from the murder. She found
him in a butcher shop, and seizing a cleaver from a rack,
flew at him like a wildcat. Alone, she subdued and held him
until her more timid associates came and secured him. And
Wild Bill had no deeper mourner than Calamity Jane. In his

passing, she lost the closest of her remaining contacts with
the scout life of the old West. His death left her more alone
and lonely, more forlorn. It left her to watch with greater
desolation the continual disintegration of her world of the
frontier.

Calamity Jane was the heroine of many yellow-backs. In
one of these perverted affairs, she was supposed to kneel by
Wild Bill, as he lay dying, and listen to his last whisper, "My
heart was yours, from the first." The mention of this story
was always sufficient to arouse Calamity Jane to outraged
fury, and her eloquent and profane denunciation would
arrest the attention of passers-by, who would stop and group
together in attitudes of intense pleasure. Jane abhorred cheap
sentiment from the very bottom of her soul. Of which statement, the following story is given as good evidence:

Once, in her palmy days, at Deadwood, a troupe of traveling players descended on the town. An impromptu stage was
rigged up, and benches placed for the audience in one of the
convenient dance-halls. When the performance started
Calamity Jane, booted and spurred, and "toting" her artillery, marched up to the front row, and from that point of
vantage, prepared to enjoy herself. But the sickly sentimen-
tality of the love scenes became quickly unendurable. There
was too little gun-play, too few redskins and sheriffs, and far
too many "mushy" passages between the insipid, sentimental
heroine and the strutting hero. Jane stood it, however,
squirming uncomfortably in her seat, until one particularly high-flown flight of passion. Unable to control herself
longer, she leaned forward and deliberately spat the juice
from a large quid of tobacco onto the pink satin gown of the
simpering leading lady. This remedy was very, even start-
lingly, successful. From a sickly, languid girl, the heroine
was metamorphosed into a screaming harridan, raging for
Calamity's blood. The rest of the audience, not so sensitive

as Jane, and deprived of entertainment by her act, also raged.
There was a pandemonium of cat calls and shouts, trampling,
and stray shots. But Calamity Jane unslung her guns, and
marched out, contemptuous and unafraid. She had injected
the action the play lacked, and the climax was pleasing to
her.

The morning after this occurred she was compelled by the
marshal to pay for the ruined pink satin, and she was heard
to remark to the "good fellers" who gathered at the bar immediately afterward, at her request, that it was worth the
price.

Now, Calamity Jane, past fifty years of age, was an
anomalous figure. She had the lined and weather-beaten face
of an old woman, and a compact, muscular body that might
have belonged to a young woman. She was still tireless; her
step was still the springy, noiseless tread of the scout and
tracker. She could ride and shoot and work as effectively as
ever. But she was an old woman. And nobody seemed to
need her or her services any more.

Compelled to make a living, she tried touring the museums
of the East, with a lecture on herself and her life as a scout.
This attempt was a failure owing to her now habitual
drunkenness and her habit of breaking over and "shooting
up" whatever town she happened to be in when the mood
came upon her.

Next, a Mrs. Josephine Blake thought she saw in Calamity
Jane the possibility of a money-making scheme. She wrote a
pamphlet on Jane and her life. Then she took her to the Buffalo Exposition, and installed her in a cottage on the road to
the Falls. Here she was to live and sell copies of the pamphlet
to passers-by for ten cents a copy. But the sodden drunkenness in which she was sunk wrecked this scheme too.

Next, Buffalo Bill, for old times' sake, tried to help her.
He placed her in a midway show, on her promise to quit

drinking so heavily. But this promise she could not keep, and
he was compelled to let her go. He bought her a ticket back
to Livingston, Montana, and put her on the train for that
place. Here she felt more at home, and she checked her
drinking a little bit. But she was an habitual frequenter of
the saloons, and was never so happy as when perched on the
top of a beer-keg in some saloon telling stories of her youth.
Long rambling accounts, disconnected incidents, happenings
in the lives of men long dead, interspersed with maudlin tears
and foolish laughter. Flaring for an instant as of old into cold,
deadly rage at the baiting of the riffraff about her, sinking
back into lethargy in its midst. Most tragic and most pitiful.

Lewis R. Freeman, writing for the *Sunset Magazine* of
July 1922, tells of meeting her in 1902, a year before her
death. He saw her at Bozeman, Montana. She was terribly
drunk. She had strayed into town and rented a room over a
saloon, where the bartender was named "Patsy" and where
there was an outside stairway up to her room. In the hopeless
confusion of her mind, all saloons seemed to her to have outside stairways, and all bartenders to be named "Patsy." She
wept over her sad plight. Finally, through the concerted
efforts of the bartenders, "Patsy," the landmark, was located and she was stowed away, safe but helpless, for the
night. The next morning, Mr. Freeman went to see her. She
was seemingly none the worse for her experience. She was
seated on an over-turned barrel, smoking a huge black cigar.
On his request for some stories of her former life, she replied:

"Sure, I'll rattle it off for you. My maiden name was
Martha Canary . . . " In a rapid sing-song, she would
progress for a few sentences until interrupted. Then she was
compelled to begin at the first again. Left alone, she gave
quite a monologue, ending, "hoping that this history of my
life may interest you one and all, I remain yours as in the old
days, Mrs. M. B. Burke, better known as Calamity Jane."

It was her old museum lecture, the "patter" which her exhibitors had taught her.

Calamity Jane finally landed in the poor house, deserted, old, alone, a sodden failure, bereft of her friends, of her gallant youth, of hope or desire, of everything that renders life on this earth tolerable. The world had passed on unheeding and left her to pitiful, drink-fuddled dreams and memories. Is it any wonder that she drowned her sorrows?

During her last year she returned in her mind to the heyday of her youth, as old people so often do. She lived again, a fearless, tireless scout. Wild Bill, California Joe, Buffalo Bill, and others of her day—all these were with her once more, young, gay, full of life and its joy. Custer, Miles, Terry, and other commanders once more rode at her side, smiled, spoke to her. The Indian foe broke and fled under her fire. The world became once again glorious, uncomplicated, young, filled with splendid action and care-free life of camp and fort. Romance flamed anew.

And through it all the figure of Wild Bill, handsome, grave, the gallant courteous gentleman, the daring clever scout, the reckless gambler, the gay comrade, typified to her all that colorful old life. He grew to fill the greater part of her horizon. So it was that when she came to die, her last request was that she might be laid by his side for her eternal rest. And those to whom she appealed, recognizing the fitness of it, did not hesitate to promise.

Her death was twenty-seven years lacking one day, August 2, 1903, after that of Wild Bill. Her funeral was under the auspices of the "Early Black-Hill Settlers," which, as she was the first white woman to enter the Black Hills, was as it should have been.

Calamity Jane lies by the side of Wild Bill, in Mount Moriah Cemetery, at Deadwood. A simple stone marks the grave, and carries the following inscription:

MRS. MARY C. BURKE

CALAMITY JANE

DIED

AUG. 1, 1903

AGED

53 YRS.

To which should be added "The greatest of all woman scouts." But she was more than that. History marks at long intervals the passage through this world of some tragic, lonely soul—some woman, too much a man to fit into a woman's restricted life, and yet too womanly to be altogether happy in her elected sphere of action.

Elizabeth of England, Catherine of Russia, any of those great half-masculine, half-feminine queens, who thought and ruled with the brains of men, and yet were women—magnificent women, in spite of all their faults—any of them would have understood and liked plain Calamity Jane. For she was of their own type. They were moulded by their age and time, by their environments. Jane was moulded by one so different, so far removed, that comparison is almost laughable. But the fact remains, that across the gulf of centuries, of customs of class, they could have found companionship.

Elizabeth—who could plan a campaign with some great general, and then drink him under the table, who had the ability to flay some offender with a profane accuracy that would shock a tramp of this day:

Catherine—great in statecraft, ruler and destroyer of men, to whom conventional morals were unknown:

And Jane—plain Calamity Jane! Such women as these loom together in force and character against the back drop of time!

CHAPTER XXVII. · *Wild Bill's Death*

W^{HEN} the gleam of gold flamed high over the Black Hills in 1876, men and women from every corner of the earth to which the rumor flew, began to surge toward the new Mecca of the yellow metal.

Cheyenne was flooded, grew, expanded. And further away Deadwood sprang into being over night. Rough shanties, cabins, tents, saloons, gambling-dens, houses flaunting the sign of the red light. Stony, rutted roads. Summers of white alkali dust in the hot relentless glare of a blazing sun; winters of silent, ice-locked never-ending cold. Shacks sheltering "outfitting" stores, slow wagons creaking past tiny patient burros bearing huge packs. The gorgeous trappings of Indian and cowboy, the gaudy but soiled finery of the dance-hall girl. All this and more—a wild whirlpool of color and life.

At Cheyenne Wild Bill lingered on, lured, as were all, by the promise of treasure. Gold and adventure—that linked pair were both his, for the taking. In the latter part of February 1876, Wild Bill learned that Mrs. Agnes Thatcher Lake was in Cheyenne, visiting a relative, a Mr. S. L. Moyer, and his family. He arranged a meeting. It was followed in a short time by their marriage.

As to the details: the ceremony was performed in the afternoon of March 5, and a few of the intimate friends of Wild Bill were present. The service was read by a Methodist minister, a Reverend W. F. Warren, after which the bride and groom took the evening train for St. Louis. Later they went to Cincinnati. Here Wild Bill spent two weeks with his

bride. But he was restless and eager to get back and go on
to the Black Hills. The new Mrs. Hickok also realized the
necessity for haste; and so at the end of the second week Wild
Bill returned to St. Louis.

Perhaps we may digress long enough to tell of the events
leading to Wild Bill's marriage. His first meeting with Mrs.
Lake had been in August 1871 at Abilene. There is no doubt
that the two, venturesome and full of courage and life, appealed to each other. But the question of love is a very
dubious one. The marriage was the practical, sensible com-
bining of forces by two people who knew that they could be
of mutual help.

Mrs. Lake was eleven years older than Wild Bill and the
mother of a little daughter, Emma. She came of a line of
famous circus performers, was the original "Mazeppa," a
skilled tight-rope dancer, a lion-trainer, a most clever and
fearless woman. She had toured Europe, performing in Berlin
at the old Victoria Theater before Emperor William, who
had given her an autographed letter of thanks. She was well
educated and an accomplished linguist.

To return to our account of Wild Bill's activities. Having
reached St. Louis, he conceived the plan of entering the
Black Hills with a party large enough to be safe from the
molestation of Indians or rough men. Accordingly he set
about organizing a company of gold hunters, prospectors, and
adventurers who wished to go to the Black Hills. As all the
men interested recognized the dangers of traveling in small
parties, he had no difficulty in forwarding his plans.

There were two routes. The first started from Bismarck,
and the second from Cheyenne. Wild Bill considered the
second by far the safer and the less expensive. About two
hundred men, half of them from St. Louis, and the other
half from Kansas City, enlisted in the company. Wild Bill
was to be the leader. They were to depend on him for both

guidance and safety. They left Cheyenne April 12, and under his skillful leadership, reached the gold fields of the Black Hills safely early in May. Here Bill left them and returned to Cheyenne, considerably the richer for the successful termination of the scheme.

He intended to devote the money so gained to mining on his own account. As he needed a partner, his meeting at Cheyenne with his old friend, Charles Utter, Colorado Charley, was very opportune. Together they turned their steps toward Deadwood. Once there, Wild Bill located several claims and started to develop them as best he could.

Deadwood, at that time, was in the hands of its worst and most lawless element. Card-sharps, runners of crooked games, cut-throats, thieves, killers, all the riffraff of slum and gutter, swept up from slimy obscurity and swirled for the moment in filthy foam on the current. Wild Bill had not come to Deadwood to renew his old profession. He had come most peacefully, on a personal errand. Yet his fame had preceded him. There were men in Deadwood who knew his record at Hays and Abilene. Why, they questioned, could he not play his rôle again? Why should not Wild Bill be marshal of Deadwood?

The rumor grew. Bill neither affirmed nor denied it. He went quietly about his ordinary work. But the wild element of Deadwood became alarmed and uneasy. There was both fear and hatred and the lawless men in the camps plotted together. Bill had a little camp with his old friend, Charley Utter. Some accounts say they shared a little cabin, others, they had only a tent. It was located across a small creek from the town. From this point Wild Bill went out on short prospecting tours.

But for all this peaceful manner, Wild Bill never allowed an insult to stand unchallenged. Wilstach tells the following incident, which is pretty well authenticated:

"Gun fighters at that time aspired to kill any one of their number who had a superior record, and thus lay claim to the championship. One night in the Montana saloon, six gun fighters, envious of Bill's prowess, were criticising him and openly threatening that they would get rid of him. A friend of Bill's overheard this talk and reported it to him. Bill immediately put his revolvers in order, and going straight to the Montana saloon, walked up to the crowd.

" 'I understand that you cheap, would-be gun fighters from Montana have been making remarks about me,' he said. 'I want you to understand that unless they are stopped there will shortly be a number of cheap funerals in Deadwood. I have come to this town, not to court notoriety, but to live in peace, and I do not propose to stand for your insults.'

"Whereupon Bill ordered the six gunmen to stand against the wall and deliver up their guns. This they did in a sheepish manner. He then backed out of the saloon, and it was the last he heard of the Montana crowd aspiring to the championship."

But Wild Bill was never to play his great part of frontier law-bringer again. Death had pointed a fleshless finger at his final hour on the great dial and waited in impatient readiness to strike. Wild Bill had a premonition of his death. No living mortal can give the reason why, nor tell how he knew. But he did know. In his heart, a voice, too faint to be clearly understood, stirred and murmured. Wild Bill listened, puzzled, half-hearing, half-believing. Most authorities tell practically the same tale.

The following version is quoted from Coursey's *Wild Bill:*

It is a strange anomaly that Wild Bill had a presentiment, or premonition, when he entered Deadwood Gulch that it would be his last. As they came to the top of the upland divide (Break Neck Hill) and looked over into Deadwood Gulch, for the first time, Wild Bill said to Charley

Utter and his companions: "Boys, I have a hunch that I am in my last camp and will never leave this gulch alive."

"Quit dreaming!" retorted Utter.

"No, I am not dreaming," replied Wild Bill; "something tells me that my time is up, but where it is coming from I do not know as I cannot think of one living enemy who would wish to kill me."

On the evening before he was killed, he was standing up leaning against the jam of the door to the building in which he was the next day assassinated, looking downcast, when Tom Dosier asked him: "Bill, why are you looking so dumpy tonight?"

Bill replied: "Tom, I have a presentiment that my time is up and that I am going to be killed."

"Oh, poo, poo!" said Tom, "don't get to seeing things; you're all right."

Bill started leisurely up Main Street, as if meditating.

And Wild Bill wrote to his wife, Mrs. Agnes Hickok. There are several versions of the letter extant. Buel claimed to be in possession of the original document and to give a copy verbatim. It agrees with the Wilstach copy, and it is certain that he saw the letter:

DEADWOOD, DAKOTA, July 17th, 1876

My own Darling Wife Agnes:

I have but a few moments left before this letter starts. I never was as well in my life; but you would laugh to see me now—just got in from prospecting. Will go away again tomorrow. Will write again in the morning, but God knows when the letter will start. My friend will take this to Cheyenne, if he lives.

I don't expect to hear from you, but it is all the same. I know my Agnes and only live to love her. Never mind, Pet, we will have a home yet, then we will be so happy. I am almost sure I will do well here.

The man is hurrying me. Good-bye, dear wife. Love to Emma.

J. B. HICKOK.

There were various saloons in Deadwood in which it is said Wild Bill met his death. A local Deadwood newspaperman, in his story of the affair, gives it as the old Bella Union. Coursey refers to it as No. 6. Harry Young, the barkeeper at that time, calls it No. 66, and Brawn and Willard in *Black Hills Trails* say it was No. 10. Daniel Lynch, a scout in the Montana Indian Wars, refers to it as the "El Dorado."

However, most writers agree that the proprietors were Carl
Mann and Jerry Lewis, of Montana. But Buel refers to it as
"a saloon kept by Nuttall and Mann." Diamond Dick said
it was the I.X.L.

Jack McCall was the drunken, degenerate tool of more
clever men. These lawless ones, knowing that it was now or
never, used Jack McCall as the instrument placed in their
hands by an evil Providence. Jack McCall, "Broken Nose
Jack," is described by Dr. E. T. Pierce, who had every opportunity to know him:

He was the most repulsive-looking man I have ever met. He was cross-
eyed, and his nose had been broken by being struck with a six-shooter. He
told me he was raised in Louisville, Kentucky, but came to the Plains
when a youth and joined a band of buffalo hunters down on the Republican River.

As to his actual and immediate preparation for the affair,
that consisted of a conversation with Tim Brady and Johnny
Varnes, two leaders of the bad men. They stressed the fact
that if Wild Bill was appointed marshal their days were
numbered. They urged on Jack McCall the glory he might
claim as the slayer of the most famous of gunmen. They
promised him absolute immunity from punishment and
quick release if captured. They gave him twenty-five dollars
in gold dust and were to add to that one hundred and
seventy-five more, after the deed was done. And as a last
assurance, they filled him up on raw whisky, the kind that
made even a coward crazy and reckless. So fortified, he set
forth to commit the crime.

At three o'clock, Wednesday afternoon, August 2, Wild
Bill was passing the long hot hours in a friendly game of
poker. He was playing with Charley Rich, Carl Mann, and
Captain Massey, a Mississippi River pilot. That they were
enjoying themselves immensely was proved by the jokes and
laughter at the table. But Wild Bill was uneasy and worried.

As the party was arranged, he was sitting with his back to the door—a position so absolutely contrary to the caution that governed his alert and watchful habit that all his time-trained instincts were in violent rebellion. But the other men, particularly Rich, with whom he wanted to change, were teasing him. Afterwards, Rich bitterly blamed himself and said that he was responsible for Bill's death by his foolish joking.

Jack McCall entered with apparent carelessness, lounging slowly behind Bill, and toward the bar. No one paid him the slightest attention. He glanced furtively around. He moved noiselessly closer. The game continued. Suddenly he jerked out his gun, and with a strangled cry of "Damn you! Take that!" fired the fatal shot. The gun was within a yard of the back of Wild Bill's head and death was instantaneous.

Still smiling, still holding his cards lightly together, he drooped slowly forward on the table, then slid to the floor. His hour had struck. His premonitions had been most tragically fulfilled.

The bullet, which had entered the back of Wild Bill's head, came out through the cheek. It continued its course, and entered Captain Massey's left arm at the wrist, ranging upward, shattering the bone. It lodged finally in his elbow, from which it was removed by a Doctor McGowan. It is said that Massey, confused by the rapidity with which the scene had transpired, and by his pain, rushed wildly into the street screaming "Wild Bill has shot me!"

Immediately after the assassination, Jack McCall, threatening Harry Young, the bartender, with a gun and keeping the other men present "covered," backed from the room. He whirled at the door and ran to his pony. He hurled himself into the saddle but the cinch was loose and the saddle turned, throwing him to the ground. He picked himself up and took refuge in an adjacent butcher shop behind a quarter of beef.

As soon as the stunned witnesses realized what had really happened, the doors of the saloon were locked and Doctor E. T. Pierce was sent for. Writing of the affair, he says:

Now, in regard to the position of Bill's body. When they unlocked the door for me to get his body, he was lying on his side, with his knees drawn up just as he slid off his stool. We had no chairs in those days—and his fingers were still crimped from holding his poker hand. Charlie Rich, who sat beside him, said he never saw a muscle move. Bill's hand read "aces and eights"—two pair, and since that day the aces and eights have been known as the "dead man's hand" in the Western country. It seemed like fate, Bill's taking off. Of the murderer's big Colt's 45 six gun, every chamber loaded, the cartridge that killed Bill was the only one that would fire. What would have been McCall's chances if he had snapped one of the other cartridges when he sneaked up and held his gun to Bill's head? He would now be known as No. 37 on the file list of Mr. Hickok.

Calamity Jane was among the first to reach the spot, and it has already been told how, though unarmed, she boldly pursued and captured the assassin. A few reports have imputed the capture to Isaac Brown, the sheriff, but most authorities give Calamity Jane all the credit.

Deadwood was thrown into an uproar. Confusion reigned. Groups gathered, broke apart, regrouped. The cry "Wild Bill is dead; Wild Bill is dead!" sped through the town. Excitement grew. Then suddenly an ominous quiet took its place. The closer friends of Wild Bill, furious, urged lynching. Quieter ones held them back, pointing out that little was to be gained by more lawlessness. Within the hour a coroner's jury was assembled, and C. H. Sheldon appointed foreman. They rendered a verdict agreeing with the circumstances of Wild Bill's death.

The cards Wild Bill was holding when he was slain, "aces and eights, the dead man's hand"—how many a future player holding that sinister combination, in some lighted cheerful room, must have felt a prickling of his scalp as if an icy breeze fanned his hands, or some dark, cold presence, suddenly in the room, stood mocking at his shoulder.

The bullet had not marred Wild Bill's face noticeably, and in death he assumed the cold beauty of carved marble. Doctor Pierce, who as he prepared Wild Bill's body for burial, is better qualified than any other to speak, has said:

When Bill was shot through the head he bled out quickly, and when he was laid out, he looked like a wax figure. I have seen many dead men on the field of battle and in civil life, but Wild Bill was the prettiest corpse I have ever seen. His tapering fingers looked like marble.

A crude tribute, but a most sincere one.

The body of Wild Bill was taken back to the little shelter that he had left so shortly before. Here it was enclosed in a coffin, and beside it, wondering, awed, passed gambler, stately Indian, and weeping child, soiled and draggled girls, stern-eyed tight-lipped men—all the motley horde of camp and town. For life, restless, unhappy, curious, is ever drawn to gaze on death. At the time of his death, Wild Bill was aged thirty-nine years, two months, and six days.

Notices of the funeral were distributed. They read as follows:

FUNERAL NOTICE

Died in Deadwood, Black Hills, August 2, 1876, from the effects of a pistol shot, J. B. Hickok, (Wild Bill), formerly of Cheyenne, Wyoming. Funeral services will be held at Charlie Utter's camp on Thursday afternoon, August 3, 1876, at three o'clock P.M. All are respectfully invited to attend.

At three o'clock on a sunny summer day, Wild Bill was buried. His face was peaceful and serene. A slight smile lingered on his lips. His long silken hair fell back from his white brow and lay across his broad shoulders. In accord with his wish expressed long before, they placed beside him in the coffin the rifle which he loved.

There were tears. Great scouts who had shared in his life and known his comradeship; pitiful girls to whom he had shown compassion; children to whom he had given tenderness; enemies to whom he had granted forgiveness; "down and outs" whom he had helped. Many could weep at his passing.

The grave was at Ingleside, on a secluded mountain slope. Great boulders, gnarled old trees, green sod, combined to give it beauty.

A clergyman spoke a few words. He prayed. The coffin was lowered. The grave was filled. The people watched, silently. And then, they left him there in solitude.

At the head of the grave was a large stump, and crudely carved on it was the inscription:

A brave man, the victim of an assassin,
J. B. Hickok, (Wild Bill), age 39 years;
murdered by Jack McCall, Aug. 2, 1876.

The pall bearers were Charlie Rich, William Hillman, Jerry Lewis, John Oyster, Charles Young, and Tom Dosier.

As Deadwood grew and expanded, the grave at Ingleside finally became too near the town, and was threatened with violation.

Therefore in 1879 Charley Utter and Louis Schoenfield, another old friend of Bill, decided to move their comrade to a more fitting spot. A new grave was dug in Mount Moriah Cemetery, and Wild Bill's coffin taken there. The lid was removed, and his old friends were allowed to see him once more. He was absolutely unchanged. He lay as one sleeping, still smiled, as though in a pleasant dream.[1]

A second burial was held. A handsome stone, was erected by Charley Utter in memory of his old friend.

The monument erected by Charley Utter was crowned with a bust of Wild Bill. This had been carved by a wandering sculptor of very good skill, and beneath it was a raised relief of Bill's crossed pistols. This tombstone was the prey of vandals and souvenir hunters. They gradually chipped it to pieces. It was replaced in 1892 by a new headstone and a life-sized figure of Wild Bill. This latter was carved by

James H. Hiordan, a visiting artist from New York. To protect it from the fate of the first monument, a steel wire cage was placed over the tomb. On Wild Bill's monument is carved this inscription—

WILD BILL
J. B. HICKOK
KILLED BY THE ASSASSIN
JACK McCALL
DEADWOOD CITY
BLACK HILLS
AUGUST 2, 1876
PARD, WE WILL MEET AGAIN IN THE HAPPY
HUNTING GROUNDS TO PART NO MORE
GOODBYE
COLORADO CHARLIE
C. H. UTTER

And so, in the fashion, told in this chapter died "Wild Bill" Hickok. His death marked not only the loss of a brave and gentle man, but also the passing of a great epic. Wild Bill, the greatest scout of the Plains, the cool and fearless marshal of border "bad towns," the marvelous marksman, the terror of desperadoes and "bad men," was gone. And with him was gone the most vital need for a man of his type. The days of wild free frontier life were numbered. Already courts and schools and libraries, factories and stores were so close that one more eager forward move would put them and the rich life they brought, into the place of saloon and gambling-hall and dance-resort.

Wild Bill, and the period in which he lived both had played their part.

CHAPTER XXVIII · *Conviction and Execution of Jack McCall*

IN THE evening following Wild Bill's murder, a mass meeting of the citizens of Deadwood was called at Mc-Daniel's theater, to start the wheels of justice grinding. As there was no regular legal jurisdiction in Deadwood, it was necessary to appoint a court and have the trial after the fashion of the law of the frontier. The law-abiding element of Deadwood had suffered a tremendous back-wash in the death of Wild Bill. The card-sharps, the bad men, the desperadoes, all the law-bearers, had gained a point and were newly fortified in self-confidence. They knew the coming trial was to be a farce—for they had themselves so decreed it.

Judge W. S. Kuykendall was appointed presiding officer at the mass meeting. Isaac Brown, the sheriff, was given a deputy and assigned twelve men for guards on the morrow. Before the meeting adjourned Judge Kuykendall was chosen Judge for the trial to be held the next morning.

At the appointed hour, on Thursday, the meeting was called pursuant to adjournment, when the action of the preceding meeting was submitted in a report read by J. A. Swift, and adopted. Col. May was chosen to conduct the prosecution, while the prisoner selected A. B. Chapline to defend him, but as Chapline was quite ill at the time, Judge Miller was named instead. A committee of three consisting of Mr. Reed of Gayville, Joseph Harrington of Deadwood, and Mr. Cain of Montana City, was next appointed by the chair, whose duty it was to select the names of thirty-three residents from each of their respective districts, and from the names thus submitted the jury of twelve was to be drawn.

Having now completed all the necessary arrangements another adjournment was ordered until two o'clock P.M., when the trial was to begin.

At two o'clock the court reconvened in the packed theater. So dense was the crowd that the court officers and the guard surrounding the prisoner were compelled to push and thrust and struggle to attain their posts.

A contemporary writer says of the prisoner at that time. Jack McCall, as he took a seat on the right of Judge Kuykendall, presented a most forbidding appearance. He was twenty-five years of age, but dissipation and a low life had painted their stains on his ugly features. His brow was low and retreating, as a sign of his cowardly and brutal propensities, while sandy hair, small moustache and cross-eyes completed the unmistakable evidences of his villainous character. He attempted to appear indifferent and assume the role of a desperado who had been accustomed to acting such parts, but despite this effort the chicken liver he possessed made his flesh creep and the blanch and color of his cheeks come and go like a patient badly overcome with intermittent fever.

Jurors were chosen. The committee submitted the required ninety-nine names, on slips of paper. These were placed in a hat and drawn out one by one by the deputy sheriff. As the town was violently partisan, it was a difficult matter to obtain twelve men claiming to be open-minded as to the innocence or guilt of Jack McCall.

However, the dozen required were at last chosen and sworn in. Their names were—L. A. Judd, J. H. Thompson, Charles Whitehead, Edward Burke, J. J. Bumfs, L. D. Brokow, John L. Thompson, K. F. Towle, John Mann, Geo. S. Hopkins, J. F. Cooper and Alexander Travis. Charles Whitehead was made foreman.

Charles Rich, Isaac Brown, Carl Mann, George M. Shingle and Harry Young, the bartender, were all called as witnesses. Their story of the tragedy was practically identical.

Jack McCall introduced Patrick Smith, Ira For, and H. H. Pitkin as men capable of testifying to his good character and general peaceableness.

At the conclusion of the testimony the Judge asked the prisoner if he desired to make any statement. He said:

Yes, I have a few words to say . . . Wild Bill killed my brother, and I killed him. Wild Bill threatened to kill me if I ever crossed his path. I am not sorry for what I done. If I had to, I would do the same thing over again.

Perhaps some few credulous persons present believed Jack McCall. But it is a matter of doubt. Certainly the clever men who had fabricated the lie for him knew the falsity of his words. After he had spoken, the prosecuting attorney examined witnesses and Wild Bill's character as a law-abiding law-enforcing man was firmly established.

Thereupon, the defendant's counsel arose and began his herculean task of presenting the prisoner as a wronged and innocent man. He waxed eloquent over the sad fate of Jack McCall's non-existent brother. He appealed for sympathy, he almost wept. He had nothing on which to base a real argument.

His flight of fancy being concluded, Colonel May arose and made a summary of the evidence submitted. He stressed the fact that Wild Bill was not in any sense a lawless man, and that he had had no quarrel with the prisoner. In conclusion he said:

It is strange, if the prisoner has been living for years with a sworn determination to kill Wild Bill, that only two days ago he should have been pleasantly engaged playing cards with him.

The case went to the jury at six o'clock. It was out an hour and thirty minutes. But almost none of the spectators left the room.

Eleven jurors were for acquittal, one, more intelligent or more honest than his fellows, for conviction. A small fine of twenty dollars was discussed, but even these men realized how ludicrous that would be. At last the jury filed back in and the foreman delivered their finding to the clerk:

"We, the jurors, find the prisoner, Mr. John McCall, not guilty.   "CHARLES WHITEHEAD, foreman."

Jack McCall was freed at once. His colleagues crowded forward to felicitate him and point out how well they had kept their promise. They were elated. Deadwood, for the time, was still a safe and pleasant place for them. But the men who had wanted to clean up Deadwood and make it a safe, decent town, were downcast. Wild Bill, who had been their hope, was dead, and his assassin freed, acclaimed innocent. They had cause to feel depressed and disconsolate.

The next morning Jack McCall left Deadwood.

From Deadwood he went to one of two places, either Custer City, or Laramie. Equally good authorities contend for each place. However, even the supporters of Laramie seem to agree that he went to Custer City later, though he visited several towns in the interim. At Custer City, when drunk, he began to boast of his murder of Wild Bill. In drunken confidences, he derided his excuse of a brother previously slain, and so robbed himself of his only plea for mercy. It was then that the men who listened decided to act. Colonel May who, furious at the findings of the Deadwood court, had been moving heaven and earth to have Jack McCall brought to real justice, redoubled his efforts. Sometimes during the first few days of October 1876, the murderer was arrested by a Deputy U. S. Marshal. Thus Jack McCall, by his own folly, brought himself to legal trial, sentence, and death. At the preliminary hearing Marshal Balacombe was directed to take him to Yankton, where he was held to await trial for the murder of Wild Bill.

The trial was short, little more than a day. The verdict was that of murder in the first degree. The Judge sentenced McCall to death. The execution was to take place on March 1, 1877.

Immediately after the trial, the "sob squad," those sentimental morons who cannot bear to see a murderer punished, became active. They circulated petitions, they pled for commutation of the sentence, they worked frantically to obtain McCall's freedom. Signed petitions were even sent to the President of the United States. But the higher court denied further trial, and this attempted derailment of justice did not succeed.

One incident of the trial showed conclusively the opinion all men shared of Wild Bill's marksmanship. Among the questions the prosecuting attorney asked Jack McCall was this one:

"Why didn't you go around in front of Wild Bill and shoot like a man?"

"I didn't want to commit suicide," replied McCall.

On March 1, 1877, in accordance with his sentence, Jack McCall was hanged.

From the *Press* and *Dakotan* of that date is taken this account of the hanging.

At half past nine, everything being in readiness, the condemned man bade farewell to his fellow prisoners, and left his prison-house for the last time. . . . The mournful train bearing its living victim to the grave, was preceded and followed by a long line of vehicles of every description, with hundreds on horseback and on foot, all leading north, out through Broadway. Not a word was spoken during the ride of two miles to the school section north of the Catholic Cemetery, (where the scaffold had been erected). McCall continued to bear up bravely, even after the gallows loomed in full view. . . . As soon as possible after reaching the place, the prisoner mounted the platform of the gallows, accompanied by Deputy Marshal Ash. Here he evinced the same firmness and nerve that had always characterized him since his arrest and trial. He placed himself in the center of the platform, facing east, and gazed out over the throng without even a quiver of the lip. U. S. Marshal Burdick, Deputy Ash, Rev. Father Daxacher and his assistant, Mr. Curry, were the only other parties upon the platform.

Immediately the limbs of the unfortunate culprit were pinioned, when he knelt with his spiritual adviser. Turning his face toward heaven, his lips were seen to move in prayer. Upon rising he kissed the crucifix; and after the black cap had been placed over his head the U. S. Marshal placed the noose around his neck. He then said: "Wait one moment, Marshal, until I pray."

Marshal Burdick waited until he had uttered a prayer, and then ad-justed the noose, when McCall said, "Draw it tighter, Marshal."

All was now in readiness, and the assemblage of nearly one thousand persons seemed to hold their breath. It was an awful moment—the single step between life and death. At precisely fifteen minutes after ten o'clock the trap was sprung, and with the single choking expression, "Oh, God," uttered while the drop fell, the body of John McCall was dangling between heaven and earth.

There remains but one more thing to tell in connection with Jack McCall. On the day after the execution, a letter was received by United States Marshal Burdick. Its brevity is pathetically eloquent. It tells the story of the traditional "black sheep." It is given here:

LOUISVILLE, KENTUCKY, February 25, 1877.

To the Marshal of Yankton:

DEAR SIR:

I saw in the morning papers a piece about the sentence of the murderer of Wild Bill, Jack McCall. There was a young man of the name of John McCall left here about six years ago, who has not been heard from for the last three years. He has a father, mother, and three sisters living here in Louisville, who are very uneasy about him since they heard about the murder of Wild Bill. If you can send us any information about him, we would be very thankful to you.

This John McCall is about twenty-five years old, has light hair, inclined to curl, and one eye crossed. I cannot say about his height, as he was not grown when he left here. Please write as soon as convenient, as we are very anxious to hear from you.

Very respectfully,

[signed] MARY A. McCALL.

NOTES

Chapter I

[1] Some of our Eastern acquaintances begged to see Wild Bill. They sent the brakeman into the little street to ask him to come in, and they gave flowers to any bystander who they saw, requesting that they be given to the renowned scout. But the more he was pursued with messages the more he retired from sight, hiding in the little back room of one of the drinking-saloons opposite. He was really a very modest man and very free from swagger and bravado. Finally, General Custer, persuaded by pretty girls, who no one ever can resist, returned with the hero of the hour, for Wild Bill and General Custer were fast friends, having faced danger together many times.

Bill's face was confused at the words of praise with which General Custer introduced him, and his fearless eyes were cast down in chagrin at the torture of being gazed at by the crowd. He went through the enforced introduction for General Custer's sake, but it was a relief when the engine whistle sounded that released him.

Physically, he was a delight to look upon. Tall, lithe, and free in every motion, he rode and walked as if every muscle was perfection, and the careless swing of his body as he moved seemed perfectly in keeping with the man, the country, the time in which he lived. I do not recall anything finer in the way of physical perfection than Wild Bill when he swung himself lightly from his saddle, and with graceful, swaying step, squarely set shoulders and well poised head, approached our tent for orders. He was rather fantastically clad, of course, but all that seemed perfectly in keeping with the time and place. He did not make an armory of his waist, but carried two pistols. He wore top-boots, riding breeches, and dark blue flannel shirt, with scarlet set in front. A loose neck-handkerchief left his fine firm throat free. The frank, manly expression of his fearless eyes and his courteous manner gave one a feeling of confidence in his word and in his undaunted courage.

There was no question that in the affrays in which he was often engaged he dealt murderous blows and shot unerring bullets; and one of the stories others told of him, as he was not given to boasting of his prowess, was of the invasion of five men in his sleeping-room in one of the new towns, where no law was established. These desperate characters locked the door, but though Wild Bill was in bed he did not lose his presence of mind. Some one hearing the noise of the contest burst open the door, and found four of the assailants dead on the floor, and Wild Bill stretched fainting on the bed across the dead body of the fifth assassin. His appearance bore no traces of this desperate side of his life. He was "the mildest manner'd man that ever scuttled ship or cut a throat." While on duty, carrying despatches, he let no temptation lure him into the company of the carousers who acknowledged him as their king. His word was law and gospel in that little town, for even where no laws are respected the word and the will of one man, who is chosen leader is often absolute.

I had with me a detachment of white scouts or Plainsmen, and one of friendly Indians. Among the white scouts were numbered some of the most noted of their class. The most prominent man among them was "Wild Bill," whose highly varied career was made the subject of an illustrated sketch in one of the popular monthly periodicals a few years ago. Wild Bill was a strange character, just the one which a novelist might gloat over. He was a Plainsman in every sense of the word, yet unlike any other of his class. In person he was about six feet one in height, straight as the straightest of the warriors whose implacable foe he was; broad shoulders, well-formed chest and limbs, and a face strikingly handsome; a sharp, clear, blue eye, which stared you straight in the face when in conversation; a finely-shaped nose, inclined to aquiline: a well-turned mouth, with lips only partially concealed by a handsome moustache. His hair and complexion were those of the perfect blond. The former was worn in uncut ringlets falling carelessly over his powerfully formed shoulders. Add to this figure a costume blending the immaculate neatness of the dandy with the extravagant taste and style of the frontiersman, and you have Wild Bill, then as now the most famous scout on the Plains. Whether on foot or on horseback, he was one of the most perfect types of physical manhood I ever saw. Of his courage there could be no question; it had been brought to the test on too many occasions to admit of a doubt. His skill in the use of the rifle and pistol was unerring; while his deportment was exactly the opposite of what might be expected from a man of his surroundings. It was entirely free from all bluster and bravado. He seldom spoke of himself unless requested to do so. His conversation, strange to say, never bordered either on the vulgar or blasphemous. His influence among the frontiersmen was unbounded; his word was law; and many are the personal quarrels and disturbance which he has checked among his comrades by his simple announcement that "this has gone far enough," if need be followed by the ominous warning that when persisted in or renewed the quarreller "must settle it with me."

Wild Bill is anything but a quarrelsome man; yet no one but himself can enumerate the many conflicts in which he has been engaged, and which have almost invariably resulted in the death of his adversary. I have a personal knowledge of at least half a dozen men whom he has at various times killed, one of these being at the time a member of my command. Others have been severely wounded, yet he always escapes unhurt. On the Plains every man openly carries his belt with its invariable appendages, knife and revolver, often two of the latter.

Wild Bill always carried two handsome ivory-handled revolvers of the large size; he was never seen without them. Where this is a common custom, brawls or personal difficulties are seldom if ever settled by blows. The quarrel is not from a word to a blow, but from a word to the revolver, and he who can draw and fire first is the best man. No civil law reaches him; none is applied for. In fact there is no law recognized beyond the frontier but that of "might makes right." Should death result from the quarrel, as it usually does, no coroner's jury is impanelled to learn the cause of death, and the survivor is not arrested. But instead of these old-fashioned proceedings, a meeting of citizens takes place, the survivor is *requested* to be present when the circumstances of the homicide are inquired into, and the unfailing verdict of "justifiable," "self-defence," etc., is pronounced, and the law stands vindicated.

That justice is often deprived of a victim there is not a doubt. Yet in all of the many affairs of this kind in which Wild Bill has performed a part, and which have come to my knowledge, there is not a single instance in which the verdict of twelve fair-minded men would not be pronounced in his favor.

CHAPTER III

[1] In accounts more picturesque than truthful Wild Bill's landing from the *Imperial* is most thrillingly told. It is also stated that: General James H. Lane was stationed at Leavenworth with a force of Free-State men called "Red Legs." In a drill of marksmanship, Bill drew from his pocket a small pistol and shot a crow which was flying overhead, then replaced his weapon without any remark. The Free-State forces set up a wild cheering and General Lane predicted that Bill would one day excite the wonder and admiration of America. As a sort of celebration of this event, Bill was named "Shanghai Bill," and was ever afterwards known by the name of "Bill." It is stated that he served under General Lane for two years.

All this is ridiculous. General Lane never had any military headquarters at Leavenworth. The "Red Legs" were not organized until the beginning of the Civil War, some six years after the landing of Bill. The Free-State people did not maintain a regular force, but assembled for military service when driven to extremity by invasions of Border Ruffians from Missouri. It is very probable that Bill did not see General Lane for some time after his arrival in Kansas.

CHAPTER V

[1] Stanley said:

The following dialogue took place between us: "I say, Mr. Hickok, how many white men have you killed to your certain knowledge?" After a little deliberation, he replied, "I suppose I have killed considerably over a hundred." "What made you kill all those men? Did you kill them without cause or provocation?" "No, by heaven! I never killed one man without good cause." "How old were you when you killed the first white man, and for what cause?" "I was twenty-eight [twenty-one] years old when I killed the first white man, and if ever a man deserved killing he did. He was a gambler and counterfeiter, and I was then in a hotel in Leavenworth City, and seeing some loose characters around, I ordered a room, and as I had some money about me, I thought I would retire to it. I had lain some thirty minutes on the bed when I heard men at my door. I pulled out my revolver and bowie knife, and held them ready, but half concealed, and pretended to be asleep. The door was opened, and five men entered the room. They whispered together, and one said, 'Let us kill the son of a ——; I'll bet he has got money.' Gentlemen, that was a time—an awful time. I kept perfectly still until just as the knife touched my breast; I sprung aside and buried mine in his heart, and then used my revolvers on the others right and left. One was killed, and another was wounded; and then, gentlemen, I dashed through the room and rushed to the fort, where I procured a lot of soldiers, and returning to the hotel, captured the whole gang of the..., fifteen in all. We searched the cellar and found eleven bodies buried in it—the remains of those who had been murdered by those villains." Turning to us, he asked, "Would you not have done the same? That was the first man I killed, and I never was sorry for that yet."

Stanley saw Wild Bill often during the service of General Hancock in Kansas, and he undoubtedly had some statement on this subject from him. Hickok must have killed a man or men in Leavenworth at that time in self-defense, as Stanley says. See statement of Mrs. Custer in first Chapter. She says he killed five men.

[2] A freight-train usually carried 200,000 pounds of goods, and after 1850 the freight from Kansas City to Santa Fé was eight dollars per hundred. That was the average. Some things were billed at much higher rates, and others at lower rates. Two hundred thousand pounds of freight at eight dollars per hundred meant that the train would earn $16,000 going from Kansas City to Santa Fé. In 1850 and thereafter teamsters were paid about twenty dollars per month, and were furnished their meals.

CHAPTER VI

[1] "History of Watauga County, North Carolina, with sketches of prominent families," by John Preston Arthur, Richmond, Va. Everett Waddey Co., 1915.

CHAPTER VII

[1] Captain William H. Gregg and "Babe" Hudspeth of Quantrill's band, and James Peacock, a soldier under Doniphan who had killed the Ruffian "Jim Crow" Chiles were some of the residents of Independence with whom the author talked of this matter.

C. F. Gross, who was one of Hickok's most intimate friends in Abilene, wrote J. B. Edwards: "I asked Bill how he came by the name of Wild Bill. Bill's answer was that a woman in Missouri during the war gave him the name."—Letter of Edwards to the author, January 27, 1926.

CHAPTER VIII

[1] From letter of H. D. Hickok:

My brother told me he was scared once when scouting. He was trying to locate a masked battery which opened fire the minute he discovered it. He, never having been under artillery fire before, said he was actually scared. The fire of that artillery brought on the battle of Wilson's Creek.

The officers knew that a battery had been placed in his vicinity. He was ordered to locate it and was advancing on it when it opened on his line. Here is a quotation from *Harper's Magazine* article: "In all your wild, perilous adventures," I asked him, "have you ever been afraid?"

"I think I know what you mean, Sir, and I'm not ashamed to say that I have been frightened. It was at the Wilme [misprint for Wilson] Creek fight. It was the first time I was ever under artillery fire, and I was so frightened that I couldn't move for a minute or so, and when I did go back the boys asked me if I had seen a ghost."

CHAPTER IX

[1] Garland Hurt lived before the Civil War in Johnson County, Kentucky. He became interested in the lead mines of Southwest Missouri. There were associated with him men from Eastern Kentucky, one named Allen, one named Stone, and others.

When Hurt abandoned lead mining, these men remained in the Southwest, some of them drifting into the Cherokee Nation. Allen married a Cherokee. She was a beautiful girl of intelligence and some education. One day a friend said: "You ought to talk to Mrs. Allen. Her husband was one of the most daring scouts in the Civil War."

The writer sought an interview with her. In 1861 it was impossible for Stone or Allen to remain in the Cherokee Nation. They went into Missouri and became connected with the Union Army. Allen was killed while riding out of the rebel lines with Wild Bill, at Prairie d'Ane.

CHAPTER X

[1] In *Heroes of the Plains* it is stated that Hickok killed thirty-five of the enemy in four hours, shooting from behind a log in Cross Timbers Hollow, and that one of these men was General McCulloch. Cross Timbers Hollow is more than two miles from Leetown, just north of which General McCulloch was killed. This statement of Buel is preposterous. General McCulloch was killed by Peter Pelican, of Company "B," Thirty-Sixth Illinois Infantry, and his death was on the seventh.

CHAPTER XI

[1] Here is the story of Black Nell found in print. It is not entirely accurate, though there is much of truth in it:

A cry and murmur drew my attention to the outside, when I saw Wild Bill riding up the street at a swift gallop. Arrived opposite to the hotel, he swung his right arm around. Black Nell instantly stopped and dropped to the ground. Bill left her there, and joined the group on the porch.

"Black Nell hasn't forgot her old tricks," said one.

"No," answered the scout. "God bless her! That mare will do anything for me. Won't you Nelly?"

The mare winked affirmatively the only eye we could see.

"Wise!" continued her master; "why, she knows more than a judge. I'll bet the drinks for the party that she'll walk up these steps and into the room and climb up on the billiard table and lie down." [At Leavenworth, after the Civil War, she performed this trick.—W.E.C.]

The bet was taken at once. Bill whistled in a low tone. Nell instantly scrambled to her feet, walked toward him, put her nose affectionately under his arm, followed him into the room, and to my extreme wonderment climbed upon the billiard table. When she got down from the table, Bill sprang upon her back, dashed through the high wide doorway, and at a single bound cleared the flight of steps and landed in the middle of the street. The scout then dismounted, snapped his riding-whip, and the noble beast bounded off down the street, rearing and plunging to her own intense satisfaction, and then quietly trotted to her stable.

"Black Nell has carried me along through many a tight place," said the scout, as we walked toward my quarters. "She trains easier than any animal I ever saw. That trick of dropping quick which you saw has saved my life time and again. When I have been out scouting on the prairie or in the woods I have come across parties of rebels, and have dropped out of sight in the tall grass before they saw us. One day a gang of rebs who had been hunting for me, and thought they had my track, halted for half an hour within fifty yards of us. Nell laid as close as a rabbit, and didn't even whisk her tail to keep the flies off, until the rebs moved off."— *Harper's Magazine,* February, 1867, pp. 279, 280.

² "I can't tell the thing as it was," said the young officer. "It was beyond description. We noticed two men ride out from the center of their line and move toward us. We saw quite a commotion all along the enemy's front, and then they commenced firing at the two riders, and then their line was all enveloped with smoke, out of which horsemen dashed in pursuit. The two riders kept well together, coming straight for us. Then we knew they were trying to escape. I watched the pursuit and their pursuers, and found the two men had halted at what I could now see was a deep wide ditch. In the face of that awful fire they deliberately turned back to get space for a good run at the ditch. This gave time for two of their pursuers to get within a few yards of them, when they stopped, evidently in doubt as to the meaning of this retrograde movement. But they did not remain long in doubt, for the two men turned again, and with a shout, rushed for the ditch, and then we were near enough to see that they were Wild Bill and his mate. Bill's companion never reached the ditch. He and his horse went down together and did not rise again. [He reached the stream and was killed as he was going over it.—W.E.C.]

"I never saw a more magnificent sight. Bill gave the mare her head, and turning in his saddle fired twice, killing both of his pursuers, who were within a few lengths of him. They went out of their saddles like stones, just as Black Nell flew into the air and landed safely on our side of the ditch. In a moment both the daring scout and the brave mare were in our midst, while our men cheered and yelled like mad."
—*Harper's Magazine,* February, 1867.

In describing this incident, the writer has followed Governor Samuel J. Crawford. He was present in the Union lines and saw Wild Bill come in.

CHAPTER XVI

¹ Told the author by Colonel H. C. Lindsay. This is only one of many adventures of Wild Bill in his service for General Hancock. Colonel Lindsay knew the men who were scouting under Hancock with Wild Bill, and he said that they were compelled to hide by day and ride by night. This is confirmed by a statement found in *Harper's Weekly,* June 29, 1867, where it is said:

These men prefer to ride at night rather than during the day. The Indians, they say, are not usually on the watch at night, and if they are, they have just as good a chance of seeing the Indians as the Indians have of seeing them. Atkins and Kinkade have both been shot at and chased by Indians during the present campaign night after night. The position of courier is one of such great danger that few men care to hold it for any length of time. "Wild Bill" is at present one of General Hancock's couriers.

[2] In describing General Hancock's Indian campaign, my father, William Elsey Connelley, in his manuscript wrote very fully of the various engagements and orders given.

In going over the book and condensing some parts I have taken the liberty of leaving out a large part of General Hancock's Indian campaign, but I have left my father's conclusions as to his ability in Indian warfare, for the reasons that I know that my father very carefully investigated that campaign and that his conclusions were reached after years of careful study and after interviewing many persons who had taken an active part with General Hancock in this campaign.

Chapter XVIII

[1] The work done by Wild Bill at this time was scattered over a vast country. General Sheridan organized a column at Fort Bascom, New Mexico, one under General Carr at Fort Lyon, Colorado, and one under Custer. General Penrose was already out. He and General Carr were to operate along the main Canadian and south to the head waters of Red River.

Wild Bill was the scout selected to keep General Sheridan in touch with these forces as the campaign progressed. At the time of the battle of the Washita he was with Carr and Penrose on the Canadian. For a disposition of forces for the campaign, see report of General Sheridan, *House Documents*, Second Session Forty-first Congress. Vol. I, 1869–70, pp. 44 *et seq.*

Chapter XIX

[1] There is some conflict in the authorities as to whether Wild Bill was at Fort Lyon in 1868 or in 1869. In a letter to the author from William L. Simpson, Thermopolis, Wyoming, it is stated that his father and mother knew Wild Bill, the acquaintance dating from 1868, at Fort Lyon.

In *Buffalo Days*, by Colonel Homer W. Wheeler, page 257, is the following: "I first met Wild Bill (James Butler Hickok) at Fort Wallace, Kansas, in the fall of 1869."

Colonel Wheeler is wrong as to the date. It was in the fall of 1868 that the Fifth Cavalry and Cody and Wild Bill went to Fort Lyon. Cody himself told the author that he and Wild Bill were there in the winter of 1868–69.

[2] Cody was at Fort Lyon when Wild Bill was brought in. He visited the scene of the fight. Wild Bill gave Cody the spear with which he had been wounded, and it was still in his possession, June 25, 1914.

Chapter XXIII

[1] In *The Life of Ben Thompson*, by the attorney who defended him for many murders, there is a vicious, slanderous indictment of Abilene and of Wild Bill. Thompson was principal owner of the Bull's Head Saloon, operated by Phil Coe. It is charged in this book that Abilene robbed the Texas cattlemen and that Wild Bill was the instrument through which the extortion was accomplished. Also that Phil Coe's mistress was assaulted and slapped or kicked by Wild Bill. Wishing to know the attitude of honest cattlemen, the author inquired of them as to the truth

or falsity of the charges set down by Thompson's biographer. These Texans repudiated these statements. Captain J. B. Gillette, banker, Marfa, Texas, is one of those of whom inquiry was made. He says there is no truth in what the Thompson book contains on that subject. Many Texans have words of praise for Wild Bill.

Chapter XXVI

[1] In *Calamity Jane and the Lady Wildcats*, by Duncan Aikman, 1927, it is stated that Jane's father died in Montana. And it is, he says, uncertain when or where her mother died. But by this account Calamity Jane was in Salt Lake City by the end of 1867. Mr. Aikman's book is written in a sneering and incredulous style. It is derisive and ironical and not to be depended on for historical accuracy in all matters.

Chapter XXVII

[1] It has been stated that Wild Bill's body, when removed from the grave at Ingleside, was in the process of petrifaction.

However, this theory is contradicted by many writers. One of these latter, writing for the *Deadwood Telegram* of November 3, 1922, states that at the time the body was taken from the grave, the people present were amazed to find:

That by some natural embalming process of the soil, accomplished by water which had percolated through the coffin, the body of Wild Bill had been so well embalmed as to preserve even the outlines of his features and the lines of the manifold pleatings of the dress shirt which he wore. This preservation of the body gave rise to the report that it had been petrified, but Mr. McClintock states that from his examination he would call it an embalming rather than a petrification, by the deposition of minerals in the tissues of the body.

INDEX OF NAMES AND PLACES